AS/400 Communications Desk Reference

1994 Edition

Compiled by

Kris Neely

Midrange Computing
5650 El Camino Real
Suite 225
Carlsbad, CA 92008

COPYRIGHT © 1993 Midrange Computing
All rights reserved. No part of this publication may be reproduced in any form without prior permission of the copyright owner.

DISCLAIMER
Every attempt has been made to provide correct information. However, the publisher does not guarantee the accuracy of the book and does not assume responsibility for information included or omitted from it.

ISBN: 1-883884-00-4

Midrange Computing
5650 El Camino Real, Suite 225
Carlsbad, CA 92008

Contents

Definitions **1-167**

Appendix A Units of Measure 169

Appendix B Conversions 171

Appendix C American Wire Gauge Sizes & Resistances 173

Appendix D Magnitude Prefixes 175

Appendix E Electronic Industries Associatio (EIA)
RS-232 Modem-Terminal Interface 177

Appendix F Commonly Referenced Standards
Organizations 179

Appendix G Selected Major Standards and
Recommendations 181

Appendix H Commonly Used North American
Carrier Systems 201

Preface

Anyone involved in the world of IBM midrange communications has had to deal with the constant blizzard of acronyms, terms and buzzwords associated with this difficult and complex field. This book is intended to put an end to this time-consuming and frustrating exercise. Over the past few years, I have patiently collected books, magazines, periodicals, brochures and advertisements in an attempt to collect as many telecommunications terms as possible to be included in this book. Much reviewing, revising and synthesizing of the definitions found has preceded this work. It does not pretend to be the final source on data- and tele-communications. Every day brings new terms, standards and technological innovations that require definitions in order to be useful in the "real world." I have tried to include as many of the definitions as I could that are relevant to the world of IBM midrange data communications. Doubtless I've forgotten some. My aim is to expand this book every year as I uncover new terms; your help is invited. If you come across a term that you think should be included in future editions, I invite you to send them to me here at Midrange Computing. You can reach me at:

Kris Neely, Connectivity Editor
Midrange Computing
5650 El Camino Real, Suite 225
Carlsbad, CA 92008-9711

FAX: 619-931-9935
BBS: 619-931-9909

A

A-B SWITCH - in data communications, a device permitting a communications line to be attached to more than one line.

A-D CONVERSION - see *Analog-to-Digital conversion.*

ABANDON CALL TIMER - a timer that instructs telephone equipment to discontinue calling attempts to another telephone.

ABATS - see *Automatic Bit Access Test System.*

ABM - see *Asynchronous Balanced Mode.*

ABORT SEQUENCE - a sequence of events which terminates the transmission of data prematurely.

ABSOLUTE BANDWIDTH - range of frequencies that a system can respond to or transmit.

ABSORPTION - a term used in fiber optics to indicate the attenuation of the light signal by the fiber-optic medium. The same concept as resistance in an electrical system.

ABSTRACT SYNTAX NOTATION ONE - used in TCP/IP network management specifications and in OSI standards as the language used for defining datatypes.

ACCESS CHANNEL CONTROL - the group of protocol devices and logic devices managing data transfer between link stations and their medium-access control layers.

ACCESS CODE - a character sequence such as a password that validates a user to a system or network.

ACCESS CONTROL - that facility which defines a user's data access privileges.

ACCESS CONTROL BYTE - an IBM term describing the byte following an IBM Token-Ring frame's or token's start delimiter. It controls access to the Token-Ring.

ACCESS METHOD - the rules that govern how computers and other devices on a network can send information through a shared physical medium in an orderly fashion. Examples include the IEEE 802 standard medium access procedures such as CSMA/CD (IEEE 802.3) and Token-Ring (IEEE 802.5).

ACCESS POINT - that location in a network where attachment capabilities are provided.

ACCESS PRIORITY - in an IBM Token-Ring environment, the maximum priority a received token can possess for the adapter to use it for transmission.

ACCESS TIME - a term widely used in local area networking to indicate the average duration from the beginning of a request for network access to the receipt of the first bit of the transmission.

ACCOUNT NETWORK MANAGEMENT PROGRAM (ANMP) - software that collects and reports information about network users and resources.

ACCUMASTER INTEGRATOR - an AT&T network management tool that collects and reports network information produced by AT&T's Network Management Protocol (NMP).

ACCUNET - an AT&T product offering comprised of a series of TI and T2 digital data services including 56Kbps service, Tl.5 service, etc.

ACF - see *Advanced Communications Functions*.

ACF/NCP - see *Advanced Communications Function/Network Control Program*.

ACF/TCAM - s e e *Advanced Communications Function/Telecommunications Access Method*.

ACF/VTAM - s e e *Advanced Communications Function/Virtual Telecommunications Access Method*.

ACF/VTAME - s e e *Advanced Communications Function/Virtual Telecommunications Access Method Entry*.

ACK - see *acknowledge*.

ACK0/ACK1 - characters used in bisync transmissions to indicate a positive acknowledgment. ACK0 and ACK1 are sent alternately to allow for the location of missing messages.

ACKNOWLEDGE (ACK) - a control character transmitted by a receiver as a positive response to a sender.

ACOUSTIC COUPLER - a device for transmitting and receiving data over a telephone line utilizing a standard telephone handset.

ACS - see *Asynchronous Communications Server*.

ACSE - see *Association Control Service Element*.

ACTIVE HUB - term used in TCP/IP networking to indicate the protocol used to determine the attachment-point address of a host to a network for the purpose of obtaining its Internet address.

AS/400 Communications Desk Reference

ACTIVE MONITOR - an IBM term used in IBM Token-Ring networks. The capacity in a single adapter that initiates token transmission and provides token error recovery capability.

ACTIVE OPEN - action initiated by an application to begin a TCP connection.

ACTIVE RELAY NODE - a network node that functions as a relay point for messages whose destination is elsewhere on the network.

ACTIVE/PASSIVE DEVICE - any device capable of supplying required current for the loop (active) and/or any device that must draw its current from equipment attached to it (passive).

ACU - see *Automatic Call Unit*.

ADAPTER SUPPORT INTERFACE - an IBM term used to describe the software which provides the common application program interface and operates IBM local area network cards in personal computers.

ADAPTIVE DELTA MODULATION (ADM) - a variation of pulse code modulation in which only the difference between signal samples is encoded.

ADAPTIVE DIFFERENTIAL PULSE CODE MODULATION (ADPCM) - a version of pulse code modulation where amplitudes are represented by four-bit values. Normally associated with a 32Kbps data transfer rate.

ADAPTIVE EQUALIZATION - a feature found on many modems which allows the modem to adapt to changes in signal distortion automatically.

ADAPTIVE PULSE CODE MODULATION (APCM) - a modulation methodology designed to carry both digital and video signals.

ADAPTIVE ROUTING - a network routing scheme that is capable of adapting to changes in traffic patterns, congestion, failures and other dynamic factors.

ADCCP - see *Advanced Data Communications Control Protocol*.

ADDED-DIGIT FRAMING - an extra character signifying the beginning and/or end of a transmission frame.

ADDRESS - 1) the 16-bit value which uniquely identifies a subarea and an element within an SNA network; 2) a value used to uniquely identify a secondary station on a multipoint data link.

ADDRESS FILTERING - a networking function in which a particular bridge permits addresses of other networks to pass through unmodified to another bridge while simultaneously identifying the addresses of that bridge's subnetworks.

ADDRESS MASK - the 32-bit binary number used to pinpoint the parts of an IP address that are used for both network and subnetwork numbers.

ADDRESS RESOLUTION PROTOCOL (ARP) - a protocol which, when given the IP address of a system, will dynamically discover the physical address of that system.

ADDRESSING - a scheme for identifying the sending and destination devices for any given item of information traveling on a network.

ADM - see *Adaptive Delta Modulation*.

ADMINISTRATIVE DIRECTORY MANAGEMENT DOMAIN - as found in the CCITT X.400 electronic mail specification, it refers to a public directory of the domains contained within a network.

ADPCM - see *Adaptive Differential Pulse-Coded Modulation*.

ADVANCED COMMUNICATIONS FUNCTION/NETWORK CONTROL PROGRAM (ACF/NCP) - an IBM software product, resident in an IBM mainframe communications controller, which controls communications between the host system(s) to which the controller is attached and the other devices attached to the network.

ADVANCED COMMUNICATIONS FUNCTION/TELECOMMUNICATIONS ACCESS METHOD (ACF/TCAM) - a subsystem operating as an ACF/VTAM applications program controlling functions such as message handling and data queuing.

ADVANCED COMMUNICATIONS FUNCTION/VIRTUAL TELECOMMUNICATIONS ACCESS METHOD (ACF/VTAM) - an IBM term referring to a system program running on IBM mainframe computers which controls communications between host-based applications and terminals.

ADVANCED COMMUNICATIONS FUNCTION/VIRTUAL TELECOMMUNICATIONS ACCESS METHOD ENTRY (ACF/VTAME) - an obsolete version of ACF/VTAM whose functions have been incorporated within current releases of ACF/VTAM.

ADVANCED COMMUNICATIONS FUNCTIONS (ACF) - an IBM term for products which support SNA functions.

ADVANCED DATA COMMUNICATIONS CONTROL PROTOCOL (ADCCP) - an ANSI application of a bit-oriented, symmetrical protocol founded on IBM's SDLC protocol. Widely used in U.S. government applications.

ADVANCED INTELLIGENT NETWORK (AIN) - a term used by common carriers in reference to any future architecture which is digital in form. AIN designs often include services such as virtual networking, voice mail and digital facsimile.

ADVANCED INTERACTIVE EXECUTIVE (AIX) - IBM's implementation of UNIX.

ADVANCED NETWORK DESIGN AND MANAGEMENT SYSTEM (ANDMS) - a database-oriented network configuration and analysis system.

ADVANCED PEER-TO-PEER NETWORKING (APPN) - an IBM term that refers to the capacity of two (or more) midrange or microcomputer systems to communicate with each other without utilizing any other higher-level SNA devices.

ADVANCED PROGRAM-TO-PROGRAM COMMUNICATIONS (APPC) - an IBM term denoting the interface which allows two programs running on different machines to communicate with each other.

AFI - see *Authority and Format Identifier.*

AGENT - a process working under SNMP which is capable of reporting alarm information, responding to get and set requests and sending trap messages.

AGGREGATE DATA RATE - the maximum quantity of data which can be transmitted over a single channel in a specific unit of time.

AIN - see *Advanced Intelligent Network.*

AIX - see *Advanced Interactive Executive.*

ALERT - an IBM term used in the SNA environment to indicate a record sent to a focal point to identify a problem.

ALERT CONTROLLER DESCRIPTION - the description of the controller to which alert messages will be sent. See *alert.*

ALERT DESCRIPTION - an SNA term referring to the information in an alert table that defines the contents of an alert for a particular message ID. See *alert.*

ALERT FOCAL POINT - the network point that processes alert messages. See *alert.*

ALERT TABLE - an object containing the definitions of SNA alerts.

ALGORITHM - refers to a specific series of logical, mathematical or procedural steps that comprise a method for solving a given problem.

ALIAS - an alternate name by which an adapter may be known to a given network.

ALLOCATION - a term used in broadband networks that refers to the assignment of a specific band of frequencies for various communications uses.

ALPHANUMERIC - in data communications, a character that is either a letter or a number.

AMERICAN NATIONAL STANDARDS INSTITUTE (ANSI) - a nonprofit body of more than 1,000 trade organizations, professional societies and companies. ANSI is the American representative at the ISO.

AMERICAN STANDARD CODE FOR INFORMATION INTERCHANGE (ASCII) - a code system that defines the bit composition of 128 different characters and symbols. Eight bits are used--seven for symbol identification and the eighth for parity.

AMERICAN TELEPHONE AND TELEGRAPH (AT&T) - in the United States, the largest supplier of long lines communications services. AT&T also owns Western Union Telegraph Company.

AMERICAN WIRE GAUGE (AWG) - the standard for measurement of the thickness of metal wire in the United States. In this system of measurement, the AWG number increases as the metal wire diameter decreases.

AMPLIFIER - a device used to increase the power of a signal--including signal characteristics and noise.

AMPLITUDE - refers to the magnitude of a sine wave.

AMPLITUDE JITTER - a common form of signal distortion characterized by a signal moving quickly from one amplitude to another.

AMPLITUDE MODULATION - the method of changing the amplitude of a carrier wave to transmit data signals. The modulation is achieved by varying the power of the signals' transmission.

AMPLITUDE NOISE - unwanted changes in the amplitude of a transmitted signal.

AMPLITUDE SHIFT KEYING (ASK) - referring to that form of amplitude modulation in which two binary values are used to modulate a given carrier signal to two different amplitudes.

AMPLITUDE-PHASE REPRESENTATION - a representation of the harmonic structure of complex signals so that there is only one amplitude and phase at each harmonic frequency.

ANALOG BRIDGE - an interface used in broadband local area networks that joins two similar networks at the channel frequency level.

ANALOG COMMUNICATIONS CHANNEL - a channel which utilizes a given band of frequencies for the transmission of data using analog signaling techniques.

ANALOG DATA - data that is constant and infinitely variable.

ANALOG REPEATER - an amplification device whose role in an analog network is to reshape, amplify and retime an incoming analog signal and then retransmit it.

ANALOG SIGNAL PARAMETERS - referring to those characteristics of an analog signal which can be controlled in order to convey information (e.g., amplitude, frequency).

ANALOG TRANSMISSION - a transmission in which data processing digital signals are converted into waveforms for transmission over voice-grade telephone lines.

ANALOG-TO-DIGITAL CONVERSION (A-D conversion) - the process of characterizing analog signal data values as digital data or signals usually by means of sampling the analog signal at regular intervals and recoding the resultant data into binary data or signals.

ANALYZER - one of a series of data communications test devices which analyzes signals, data or a transmission medium and reports the parameters or content for the purposes of problem solving or quality control.

ANDMS - see *Advanced Network Design and Management System.*

ANGLE MODULATION - a modulation technique where the angle of a sine carrier wave is varied. Frequency Modulation (FM) is a type of angle modulation.

ANI - see *Automatic Number Identification.*

ANMP - see *Account Network Management Program.*

ANNOUNCED RETRANSMISSION RANDOM ACCESS (ARRA) - a protocol used in slotted transmission broadcast networks that provides for the reservation of a slot once a collision has occurred.

ANSI - see *American National Standards Institute.*

ANSWER MODE - the operating condition of a modem set to answer a telephone and receive data for another system.

ANSWER TONE - a tone signal with a frequency normally between 2025 and 2225 Hertz used by an answering modem to indicate its ready condition to a calling modem. The answer tone's normal duration is at least 1.5 seconds.

ANSWER/ORIGINATE - the capacity of some modems to answer incoming calls and originate outgoing calls.

ANTENNA - any device which is capable of radiating electromagnetic signals and of capturing them.

APCM - see *Adaptive Pulse Code Modulation.*

APDU - see *Application Protocol Data Unit.*

APPC - see *Advanced Program-to-Program Communications.*

APPENDAGE - In an IBM Token-Ring environment, the applications program subroutine that assists in handling various ring events.

APPLESHARE - the family of file server software available for the Apple Computer Macintosh line.

APPLETALK - Apple Computer's group of networking products.

APPLICATION ENTITY - an active service entity existing at the application layer of the OSI model.

APPLICATION LAYER - the highest layer of both the OSI reference model and of IBM's SNA model. It contains services which interface the communications system with the user.

APPLICATION PROGRAM - software that a user interacts with, or uses. Word processing programs, spreadsheet programs and IBM's MAPICS DB are examples of application programs.

APPLICATION PROGRAM INTERFACE (API) - an IBM phrase referring to an interface between one application and another. APPC uses the LU 6.2 application program interface.

APPLICATION PROTOCOL DATA UNIT (APDU) - a data structure at the application layer of the OSI reference model protocol suite which communicates application information.

APPLICATION SERVICE ELEMENT (ASE) - refers to entities as defined in the OSI reference model's application layer, which can he broken down into ASEs for the purpose of supporting specific application tasks such as file transfer or other internetworking capabilities.

APPLICATION SUBSYSTEM SNA - an IBM phrase which refers to subsystems that are either transaction (e.g., CICS) or interactive (e.g., TSO).

APPLICATIONS PROCESSOR - network nodes that provide data- or information-processing applications support.

APPN - see *Advanced Peer-to-Peer Networking*.

ARC - see *Attached Resource Computer*.

ARCHITECTURE - the plan of a network that determines how the network components will fit together.

ARM - see *Asynchronous Response Mode*.

ARP - see *Address Resolution Protocol*.

ARPANET - the world's original packet-switching network, now a part of Internet.

ARQ - see *Automatic Repeat Request* and *Automatic Request for Repeat*.

ARRA - see *Announced Retransmission Random Access*.

ARRIVAL RATE - the average rate at which information arrives at a device for processing.

AS/4OO - introduced by IBM in 1988 as the replacement midrange machine for the System/36 and System/38. The AS stands for Application System.

ASCII - see *American Standard Code for Information Interchange*.

ASCII DEVICE - refers to a start-stop type of terminal which supports ASCII coding.

ASE - see *Application Service Element*.

ASK - see *Amplitude Shift Keying*.

ASP - see *Attached Support Processor*.

ASSERTED DEVICE - an interchange circuit placed in an ON condition by a device connected to it to indicate a status or requirement to another device.

ASSOCIATION CONTROL SERVICE ELEMENT (ACSE) - referring to those elements of the OSI reference model which provide the functions necessary to manage application associations.

ASYMMETRIC PROTOCOL - any communications protocol which uses different communications parameters for transmission in each direction.

ASYNC - abbreviation of *asynchronous*.

ASYNCHRONOUS - data-transmission methodology where each character (composed of eight bits) to be transmitted is bordered by a start bit and one or more stop bits. Referred to as *async*, this method uses no timing or clocking information during transmission.

ASYNCHRONOUS BALANCED MODE (ABM) - the operational mode of a balanced data link in which stations may send commands or initiate transmissions without explicit permission from other stations.

ASYNCHRONOUS COMMUNICATIONS SERVER (ACS) - a communications server used in local area networks which allows users to dial out of the network onto the public switched telephone network or to access leased lines for asynchronous communications.

ASYNCHRONOUS RESPONSE MODE (ARM) - the capacity of a secondary station to begin transmission without permission from a primary station within a bit-oriented protocol environment.

ASYNCHRONOUS TRANSFER MODE (ATM) - a communications standard defining network services for the transmission of data within high-speed local area networks at speeds of up to 155Mbps.

ASYNCHRONOUS/SDLC - data-link level communications protocol allowing SDLC-like protocols to be transmitted over asynchronous lines.

AT&T - see *American Telephone and Telegraph*.

ATM - see *Asynchronous Transfer Mode*.

ATTACHED RESOURCE COMPUTER (ARC) - a network device available to any other network device for computational or other processing duties.

ATTACHED SUPPORT PROCESSOR (ASP) - one of the job entry subsystems used in IBM's OS/SVS operating system.

ATTACHMENT UNIT INTERFACE (AUI) - the interface between a LAN network device and a medium attachment unit. Cables are often described as AUIs.

ATTENUATION - a decrease in transmission strength between two transmission points.

ATTENUATOR - any device which intentionally manufactures attenuation.

AUDIBLE ALARM - an audible sound device used to signal a terminal operator's attention to some event or condition.

AUI - see *Attachment Unit Interface*.

AUTHORITY AND FORMAT IDENTIFIER (AFI) - a field, as defined in the ISO addressing scheme for network service access points, which identifies the type of address domain.

AUTO ANSWER - a modem feature which allows the modem to automatically answer an incoming telephone call.

AUTO CALLBACK - a feature of some modems in which an incoming call causes the modem to prompt the user for a password, validate the password, terminate the connection and then dial back the phone number of the user who placed the call.

AUTO DIAL - a feature which allows a modem to automatically dial a telephone number. The telephone number is dialed as part of a command stream.

AUTOBAUD MODEM - a family of modems which uses the first group of characters received to sense and adjust their baud rate to match that of attached devices.

AUTOMATIC BIT ACCESS TEST SYSTEM (ABATS) - an AT&T system which performs loopback tests of CSUs/DSUs.

AUTOMATIC CALL UNIT (ACU) - a device used with a standard modem to dial the telephone number for the originating equipment. Used with both asynchronous and synchronous equipment.

AUTOMATIC NUMBER IDENTIFICATION (ANI) - a user service employed by ISDN that allows the receiver of a call to see the phone number of the calling party.

AUTOMATIC POLLING - an IBM term for a communications controller capability in which terminals are polled based on their address.

AUTOMATIC REPEAT REQUEST (ARQ) - a group of protocols for the acknowledgment of the successful receipt of transmitted blocks of data. Half-duplex in nature.

AUTOMATIC REQUEST FOR REPEAT (ARQ) - a type of error control commonly used in synchronous data link protocols (e.g., IBM's SDLC) in which a receiving address automatically requests a retransmission from the transmitting address when an error is detected.

AUTONOMOUS SYSTEM - a collection of routers using a common Interior Gateway Protocol under the direction of a single administrative authority.

AWG - see *American Wire Gauge*.

B

B-ISDN - see *Broadband ISDN*.

BABBLING NODE - a network station which continuously transmits nonsense.

BACK-END LAN - networking scheme for connecting mainframes to large-scale DASD. Defined in FDDI standards.

BACK-END PROCESSOR - opposite of a front-end processor, a back-end processor is responsible for background applications functions (printing, computing, etc.) and has no direct interaction with users.

BACKBONE - the interconnecting bus of a backbone network.

BACKBONE NETWORK - any network used to connect two or more subnetworks. The backbone often has no users attached and may run at different speeds than the networks attached to it. Backbones often use different topologies and protocols than the attached networks.

BACKGROUND NOISE - base level of noise in a specific communications environment.

BACKHAUL CONNECTION - any line connecting a user to a network hub.

BACKOFF - refers to the scheme followed when there is a transmission collision in a contention-oriented access technique (i.e., Ethernet). In a collision situation where backoff is in use, each station involved in the collision ceases to transmit and waits for a backoff period of time before attempting to transmit.

BACKWARD CHANNEL - a transmission channel in a communications link used to carry network management data or error correction data. Data on backward channels travesl opposite the flow of primary communications channels.

BACKWARD ERROR CORRECTION (BEC) - error-detection scheme in which the receiver of the message detects the error condition and reports the finding to the transmitter, at which point the transmitter must retransmit the message.

BALANCED CIRCUIT - any network-terminated circuit whose impedance is balanced by the impedance of the line, resulting in little or no return loss.

BALANCED CONFIGURATION - refers to any link configuration in which end stations on the link may start transmissions without being granted permission to do so by the other end station.

BALANCED LINE - any communications line having equal resistance per unit length and equal capacitance and inductance between each conductor and electrical ground.

BALANCED TRANSMISSION - transmission mode in which signals have two separate and distinct physical paths: one outbound and one inbound.

BALANCING - the process used in broadband networks of changing the gain/loss in each path of the network in order to achieve signaling levels that are as equal as possible.

BALUN - a "BALanced to UNbalanced" connector. A physical device for connecting twisted-pair wiring to coaxial cable.

BAND - contiguous range of frequencies.

BAND SPLITTER - any of the family of multiplexers designed to separate the available bandwidth into separate channels.

BAND-LIMITED SIGNAL - any signal in which the constituent frequencies are limited to a specific range.

BANDPASS FILTER - in analog circuits, a signal-filtering device which blocks specific frequencies and permits other frequencies to pass. The tuner on your car radio is an example of this concept.

BANDPASS SIGNAL - any signal contained within a group of signals passed through a bandpass filter.

BANDWIDTH - the difference, in Hertz, between the highest and lowest frequencies of a signal. For example, if the lowest frequency is 100Hz and the highest frequency is 1100Hz, then the resulting bandwidth is 1000 Hz. The portion of frequencies available for effective transmission of data.

BANDWIDTH EFFICIENCY - a numeric value representing the ratio between data rate and bandwidth for a channel.

BARREL CONNECTOR - any physical connector which resembles a barrel. BNC connectors, for example. Used to "straight line" a connection between two similar pieces of transmission media such as coax.

BASEBAND - signal transmission scheme in which digital signals are put on the transmission medium without modulation. Bits are transmitted as voltage pulses.

BASEBAND CABLE - normally, coaxial cable used in baseband networks.

BASEBAND NETWORK - any network scheme in which baseband technology is used.

BASEBAND SIGNAL - voltage pulse which occupies the entire bandwidth of the medium it is applied to.

AS/400 Communications Desk Reference

BASIC INFORMATION UNIT (BIU) - an IBM term from SNA referring to an informational unit which is comprised of an RU and an RH added by the transmission control layer.

BASIC INPUT/OUTPUT SYSTEM (BIOS) - as defined for use in an IBM PC/DOS environment, the software/firmware services providing application-to-I/O port interface.

BASIC MAPPING SUPPORT (BMS) - an IBM term used in CICS to describe a terminal screen formatting utility.

BASIC MODE LINK CONTROL (BMLC) - as defined by the ISO and the CCITT, BMLC defines the control of a communications link via ASCII control characters.

BASIC RATE ACCESS (BRA) - refers to the initial access offering in an ISDN network. Normally, two 64Kbps B-channels and one 16Kbps D-channel. Also known as *Basic Rate Interface* (BRI).

BASIC TELECOMMUNICATIONS ACCESS METHOD (BTAM) - a term referring to IBM's communications methodology used in MVT and MFT nonvirtual storage-oriented systems. Precursor to VTAM.

BASIC TRANSMISSION UNIT (BTU) - an IBM term used in SNA networks to denote a packet of information which contains one or more Path Information Units (PIUs). An example of a BTU is the information field of an SDLC information frame.

BAUD RATE - the signaling rate of a transmission medium. Often confused with bits per second (bps), baud rate and bps are the same only in signaling schemes in which one bit is sent on one signal.

BAUDOT CODE - a five-bit communications coding scheme invented by Emile Baudot for use in teletype systems.

BBS - see *Bulletin Board System.*

BCC - see *Block Check Character.*

BCD - see *Binary Coded Decimal.*

BEACON - as defined for use in IBM's SDLC, a beacon is a frame used to detect carrier signal problems in loop transmissions. In token-ring applications, a beacon is a message used to inform the ring that token passing has ceased due to a failure somewhere in the network.

BEAM SHAPING - the process of shaping an airborne transmission signal in order to ensure that the signal covers a specific geographic area.

AS/400 Communications Desk Reference

BEAM SPLITTER - any device designed to split a single optical transmission into two or more separate optical beams.

BEARER CHANNEL (B CHANNEL) - 64Kbps channel used in ISDN.

BEC - see *Backward Error Correction*.

BELL - transmission control character used to get the attention of a human.

BER - see *Bit Error Rate*.

BERT - see *Bit Error Rate Tester*.

BGP - see *Border Gateway Protocol*.

BIAS DISTORTION - a form of signal distortion caused by having modulation periods of different lengths.

BIG ENDIAN - in data transmission, a data-formatting scheme in which the most significant byte (or bit) is placed first.

BINARY CODED DECIMAL (BCD) - communications coding scheme in which decimal digits are translated into four or six binary digits.

BINARY DATA - refers to the process of representing data with binary digits (1's and 0's).

BINARY PHASE SHIFT KEYING - any of the family of binary modulation techniques which employs phase shifting.

BINARY SYMMETRIC CHANNEL - a communications channel designed so that the probability of changes in binary bits sent in one direction is equal to the probability of changing the same binary bits back to their correct state.

BINARY SYNCHRONOUS COMMUNICATIONS (BSC, bisync) - an IBM term referring to a form of data link control protocol utilizing various framing characters to establish communications control functions. Bisync is a half-duplex, character-oriented, stop-and-wait protocol, uses EBCDIC, ASCII or transcode character sets, supports point-to-point and switched channels and is normally referred to by the terminal type being used or emulated (i.e., 2780 or 3780 bisync).

BIND - an IBM term used to designate the command transmitted from one network-addressable unit (NAU) to another, activating a communications session between them.

BINDING - an IBM term referring to the process in SNA in which BIND commands activate NAU-to-NAU sessions.

BIOS - see *Basic Input/Output System*.

BIPHASE MANCHESTER CODING - signal-coding scheme used in LANs such as Ethernet in which a low-to-high signal level, called a transition, represents a binary "1" and a high-to-low transition represents binary "0".

BIPLEXER - a form of multiplexer which has the capacity to multiplex two data streams onto a single communications link.

BIPOLAR - having both positive and negative voltages.

BIPOLAR CODING - AT&T bit-encoding scheme used for Tl or greater transmissions. In bipolar coding, opposite polarity is used to represent successive marks (1's) and a neutral state represents spaces (0's).

BIS - an additional qualifying indicator at the end of some CCITT recommendations used to show that the standard indicated is an alteration of a preexisting standard.

BISYNC - see *Binary Synchronous Communications*.

BIT - the smallest unit of information in data communications; a binary digit, either 1's or 0's.

BIT DURATION - the amount of time for one bit to pass a specific point. This time plus the time between bits, known as the interbit duration, is the inverse of the bit transmission rate.

BIT ERROR - refers to the condition in which a bit has been changed during the transmission process.

BIT ERROR PROBABILITY - a measure of the probability that a given transmitted bit will be in error.

BIT ERROR RATE (BER) - a measurement of the rate at which bit errors occur during a given transmission.

BIT ERROR RATE TESTER (BERT) - any device designed to measure the bit error rate. BERTs measure this rate by transmitting a known bit pattern and then checking the received pattern for errors.

BIT INSERTION - used in synchronous communications to insure data transparency; refers to the process of inserting a bit (normally a 0) in a data stream so that the data being transmitted contains a bit sequence which is in the same pattern as the transmission control bit sequence. Also known as *bit stuffing*.

BIT INTERLEAVING - term used in time-division multiplexing to denote the selection and insertion of data bits from multiple sources into specific, predefined slots on a multiplexed communications channel.

BIT MULTIPLEXING - bit-oriented multiplexing scheme similar in concept to bit interleaving.

BIT REPEATERS - also called *regenerative repeaters*, bit repeaters receive an incoming bit, ensure its signal integrity and transmit it onward.

BIT STREAM - any serial flow of bits on a communications line.

BIT STUFFING - any technique which intentionally inserts extra bits into a data stream in order to ensure that the transmitted data is not mistakenly identified as communications control characters. Also known as *zero-bit insertion* or one-bit insertion.

BIT SYNCHRONIZATION - any signal sampling technique which seeks to ensure that data signals are sampled at the correct interval required to determine a bit's correct value.

BIT-ORIENTED PROTOCOLS - refers to the protocols which are capable of transmitting bits transparently across a communications line with only the starting and ending flag bits having meaning. Control information is contained within specific bit patterns. IBM's SDLC is one example.

BITS PER SECOND (bps) - a measure of the speed at which bits are transmitted through a communications channel; the number of bits passing a specific point in a communications channel in one second of time.

BIU - see *Basic Information Unit* and *Bus Interface Unit*.

BLAST - see *Blocked Asynchronous Transmission*.

BLERT - see *Block Error Rate Tester*.

BLIND TRANSFER - refers to the transmission of a message to a node without benefit of prior knowledge as to whether or not the node is active.

BLOCK - any set of characters transmitted as a group. Block sizes may be fixed or variable in length.

BLOCK CANCEL CHARACTER - any transmission control character designed to indicate that all previous characters in the previous block should be discarded.

BLOCK CHECK CHARACTER (BCC) - characters transmitted with a message frame to facilitate error detection by the receiver. Examples of BCCs are *Cyclic Redundancy Check* (CRC) and *Longitudinal Redundancy Check* (LRC).

BLOCK ERROR RATE - a measure of the error rate associated with the transmission of data in blocks; a ratio of blocks with errors to total blocks.

BLOCK ERROR RATE TESTER (BLERT) - any device designed to calculate the block error rate of a communications link.

BLOCK MODE - refers to the block oriented, (normally) half-duplex operating mode of a start/stop terminal which transmits data in blocks.

BLOCK MODE TERMINAL INTERFACE (BMTI) - an X.25 Packet Assembler/Disassembler (PAD) device used with block-oriented terminal equipment to assemble and disassemble X.25 data packets.

BLOCK MULTIPLEXER CHANNEL - an IBM term used to refer to the company's mainframe I/O channel designed to permit the multiplexing of blocks of data.

BLOCK SYNCHRONIZATION - the transmission of a block of data containing synchronization data which will ensure synchronization between transmitter and receiver.

BLOCKED ASYNCHRONOUS TRANSMISSION (BLAST) - popular data communications scheme known for its error-free transmissions, in which data is transmitted in blocks and not on a character-by-character or line-by-line basis.

BLOCKING - the grouping of data transmission characters into a single message (block) for transmission.

BMLC - see *Basic Mode Link Control*.

BMS - see *Basic Mapping Support*.

BMTI - see *Block Mode Terminal Interface*.

BNC CONNECTOR - a specific type of coaxial cable connector.

BOOT NODE - any node in a network at which other nodes may download software.

BORDER GATEWAY PROTOCOL (BGP) - a TCP/IP routing protocol used for interdomain routing.

BOUNDARY NODE - an IBM term used to denote, within SNA, a subarea node which is capable of limited protocol support for adjacent subarea nodes.

BPS - see *bits per second*.

BRA - see *Basic Rate Access*.

BRACKETING - refers to the scheme of adding header and trailer control characters to a message.

BRANCH CABLE - an intermediate cable in a broadband coaxial network which either feeds to or feeds from the main trunk line.

BREAK - a space used in asynchronous communications for control purposes. Normally, a break is at least a character length in duration.

BREAKOUT BOX - a test/diagnostic device for viewing the signals in a physical interface such as RS-232.

BRI - see *Basic Rate Interface.*

BRIDGE - any device designed to connect networks at the data-link control layer of their architecture; or, devices used to connect parts of the same network. Bridges do not interpret the data they handle; they just pass it on.

BROADBAND - also known as wideband, broadband is generally referred to as any transmission scheme in which data moves from its source to its destination in a form that differs from the form it had at the source; or, the transmission of multiple analog signals over the same communications link.

BROADBAND ISDN (B-ISDN) - an ISDN service implemented on a broadband, analog transmission medium in which support is provided for bandwidths in excess of the primary rate in order to facilitate the transmission of, among other things, video and image information.

BROADCAST ROUTING - refers to any of the family of communications routing schemes in which messages are transmitted to multiple destinations, or in which a message may be transmitted multiple times to a single destination.

BROADCASTING - the transmission of messages to all or multiple network nodes at the same time.

BROUTER - any device which combines the functions of both a bridge and a router.

BSC - see *Binary Synchronous Communications.*

BTAM - see *Basic Telecommunications Access Method.*

BTU - see *Basic Transmission Unit.*

BUFFER - temporary storage space used to hold information before and after transmission.

BULLETIN BOARD SYSTEM (BBS) - a computerized facility allowing users to interact. Users of BBSs dial up the BBS to perform functions such as messaging, and data retrieval.

BURST ERRORS - any group of transmission error that occurs in groups or clusters.

BURST TRAFFIC - data transfer across a network characterized by the infrequent transmission of large volumes of data.

BUS - 1) a linear topology network; 2) an electrical circuit designed to act as a shared pathway for multiple devices.

BUS INTERFACE UNIT (BIU) - any device designed to perform as an interface between a bus and a network station.

BUS LOCAL NETWORK - any of the forms of high-speed LANs using a bus topology.

BUS TOPOLOGY - any network scheme in which all stations of the network are connected to a single cable.

BYPASS - using telecommunications services which avoid common carrier service, in order to reduce telecommunications costs.

BYTE - the number of bits (usually eight) used to represent one character.

BYTE COUNT PROTOCOLS - any of the family of communications protocols which utilize special control bytes for transmission control and incorporate a "count field" to maintain data transparency.

BYTE MULTIPLEXER CHANNEL - an IBM term referring to the I/O channel design which calls for the multiplexing of bytes of data.

BYTE MULTIPLEXING - similar to bit multiplexing, interleaving bytes instead of bits.

BYTE STUFFING - refers to the process of inserting unneeded "dummy" data bytes into a data transmission in order to bring the net data transmission rate under that of the actual channel data rate.

BYTE SYNC - the process of synchronizing a communications link on a byte-by-byte basis.

BYTE-ORIENTED PROTOCOL - any data-transmission scheme in which bytes for data are used to control transmission functions. Bisync is a byte-oriented protocol.

C

C BAND - satellite transmission frequency band from 4-6GHz.

CABLE - a group of wires or fibers encased in an insulator through which signals may pass.

CABLE KIT - an IBM term used to describe, in broadband networks, cabling components which consist of an eight-port splitter and attenuators used to connect PCs to a network.

CABLE LOSS - a measure of the amount of radio frequency signal attenuation by a coaxial cable.

CABLE TILT - a term used to describe the variation of cable attenuation with frequency.

CABLE TRAY - a plastic or metallic tray used to group transmission cables together for ease of cable management.

CALL ACCOUNTING - refers to any system for collecting and reporting, from a telephone system, information regarding the system's utilization.

CALL DETAIL RECORDING (CDR) - type of PBX which logs all calls.

CALL ROUTING - any scheme for establishing a route through a network in order to set up a path for a telephone call.

CALL SETUP - refers to the establishment of a connection between the caller and the recipient of the call, after the dialing of the last digit of the telephone number and including the call routing time.

CALL-ACCEPTED SIGNAL - signal generated by called equipment which indicates that it accepts the incoming call.

CALL-BACK UNIT - any device or software product which validates the identity of an incoming telephone caller and then hangs up and dials the caller back; used as a security measure and to reverse the charges of the call.

CALL-NOT-ACCEPTED SIGNAL - signal generated by called equipment which indicates that it will not accept the incoming call.

CAMBRIDGE RING - a type of ring network composed of twisted-pair wiring operating at 10Mbps, with repeaters every 100 meters for long-distance transmission via other media (i.e., coax, twinax or fiber).

CAMPUS AREA NETWORK (CAN) - similar to a large LAN or a small MAN. CANs are networks designed to operate within a relatively small geographic area. Backbones are used to connect each building in the CAN together.

CAN - see *Campus Area Network* and *Cancel*.

CANCEL (CAN) - control character denoting that the preceding characters are in error and are subject to cancellation.

CANM - see *Computer-Aided Network Management*.

CAPACITANCE - the ability to collect and hold an electrical charge after the termination of the electricity.

CAPACITY - the throughput (in bits per second) of a transmission circuit.

CARRIER - a steady sine signal which carries no information in and of itself. The carrier wave must be changed (modulated) in order for it to impart transmitted data.

CARRIER BAND - a term used to describe a baseband network which uses modulation to reduce unwanted line noise.

CARRIER DETECT (CD) - term (or control panel light on a modem) used in modern technology which indicates that the modem has detected a carrier signal on the line.

CARRIER DETECT CIRCUIT - circuitry used to detect the presence of a carrier wave on a transmission medium.

CARRIER FREQUENCY - usually the midpoint frequency, in cycles per second, of the bandwidth of a carrier wave.

CARRIER SENSE MULTIPLE ACCESS (CSMA) - form of data-link level networking protocol in which multiple stations on the network can transmit when the network is idle.

CARRIER SENSE MULTIPLE ACCESS WITH COLLISION AVOIDANCE (CSMA/CA) - refers to a form of CSMA in which the stations on the network inform the network via a handshaking scheme that they wish to transmit data on the network. Potential collisions are limited in this way.

CARRIER SENSE MULTIPLE ACCESS WITH COLLISION AVOIDANCE AND POSITIVE ACKNOWLEDGMENT (CSMA/CAPA) - form of CSMA which uses positive acknowledgments to eliminate collision errors.

CARRIER SENSE MULTIPLE ACCESS WITH COLLISION DETECTION (CSMA/CD) - a form of CSMA in which each station wishing to transmit data on the network waits a random amount of time before attempting the transmission, after detecting a collision on the network.

CARRIER SENSE MULTIPLE ACCESS WITH COLLISION PREVENTION (CSMA/CP) - form of CSMA used in the IEEE 802.3 specification.

CARRIER SIGNAL - see carrier.

CARRIER WAVE - see *carrier*.

CARRIER WAVE MODULATION (CWM) - the changing of a carrier by means of a modulation technique in order to convey information.

CARRIER-TO-NOISE RATIO (CNR) - a measure of the ratio of carrier-wave signal to noise in analog transmission systems.

CASCADED BRIDGES - network bridges which are hooked together in order to connect multiple network segments or entire networks.

CASCADING - refers to the process of hooking up several multiplexers so that their output becomes the input to a final multiplexer. This "cascaded" signal is then transmitted. Significant line cost savings may result. If the traffic to the input multiplexers exceeds the expectations of the final multiplexer, bottlenecks--and a resultant reduction in performance characteristics--may occur.

CASCADING FAULTS - faults in a network which trigger other network faults.

CASE - see *Common Application Service Element*.

CBMS - see *Computer-Based Message System*.

CBX - see *Computerized Branch Exchange*.

CC - see *Cluster Controller*.

CCITT - see *Consultative Committee on International Telephone and Telegraph*.

CD - see *Carrier Detect*.

CDR - see *Call Detail Recording*.

CELL RELAY - any process in which a network node relays a cell, or packet, of information, usually fixed in length, to an adjacent node in the network. Also referred to as *Frame Relay*.

CENTER FREQUENCY - (also commonly referred to as the "center freq") the center, or middle, frequency in a band of frequencies.

CENTRAL OFFICE (CO) - normally, a telephone-company office controlling the telephone-switching system for a specific geographic area.

CENTRALIZED NETWORK - another term for star networks; centralized networks have a central network node to which all other network nodes are directly attached.

CENTRALIZED RESERVATION ACCESS - refers to any access technique in which access to the medium is controlled via a master controller, which assigns time slices on the medium by means of a reservation inquiry.

CENTRONICS INFERFACE - refers to a particular type of parallel communications adapter used to connect peripheral devices together.

CERT - see *Character Error Rate Tester.*

CHAINING - the connecting together of messages, frames, cells or other data-communications data-transmission transactions, to ensure proper delivery sequence.

CHAINING PROTOCOL - an IBM term used in SNA to denote a method of logically defining and transmitting a complete unit of data.

CHANNEL - another term for line or circuit; a channel is the minimal division of a communications path capable of transmitting/receiving data.

CHANNEL ATTACHED - a communications scheme in which two devices are attached via a high-speed communications link in order to optimize communications performance between them.

CHANNEL BANK - refers to the devices which permit 24 voice grade channels to be multiplexed into a single T1 transmission line.

CHANNEL CAPACITY - maximum transmission rate of a channel.

CHANNEL GROUP - a grouping of twelve adjoining telephone channels in order to permit their multiplexing as a whole.

CHANNEL SERVICE UNIT (CSU) - telephone line interface charged with ensuring the correct shaping and timing of transmitted digital signals.

CHANNEL SLOT TIME (CST) - term used in time-division multiplexing to indicate the amount of time that each attached device has been allocated for data transmission.

CHARACTER ERROR RATE TESTER (CERT) - any test device designed to generate characters and test the error rate of said transmission.

CHARACTER INTERLEAVING - time-division multiplexing scheme for interleaving characters rather than bits for transmission.

CHARACTER ORIENTED PROTOCOL - any data-link protocol which relies on characters to manage transmission. Contrast to *bit-oriented protocols*.

CHARACTER STUFFING - character stuffing is normally used in a bisynchronous protocol to allow the transmission of any character (including control characters) in a message frame; similar to bit stuffing.

CHARACTER SYNCHRONIZATION - refers to any scheme which permits a receiving device to decide which bit groupings may be assembled into characters.

CHARACTER-CODE CONVERSION - the translation by a receiving device of one character set into another. ASCII-to-EBCDIC conversion would be an example of this.

CHARACTERISTIC IMPEDANCE - termination impedance of a balanced line that will reduce end-to-end signal reflection.

CHARACTERS PER SECOND (cps) - measure of the transmission rate of a communications medium expressed in the number of characters per second which may be transferred on the medium.

CHEAPERNET - slang term used for thin Ethernet cable based on 802.3 standard networks. Thin Ethernet cable is rated to 185 meters, normal. Ethernet cable is rated to 500 meters.

CHECK DIGIT - digit attached to the end of a string of characters in order to warrant its accuracy. Also known as a check character, this technique represents a simplistic error-checking mechanism.

CHECKSUM - an error-detection control character. See *Block Check Character* and *Cyclic Redundancy Check*.

CICS - see *Customer Information Control System*.

CIRCUIT - any path on a communications channel which connects two or more devices.

CIRCUIT SWITCHING - any scheme for creating a link in a network between transmitting and receiving stations. The link may be physical (as in physical circuit-switching schemes) or logical (as in virtual circuit-switching techniques). Normally, the link is established only for the time required for the communications session.

CIRCUIT-SWITCHED DATA NETWORK (CSDN) - refers to any network which, by means of a circuit-switching scheme, sets up a channel between two or more network devices.

CIU - see *Communications Interface Unit*.

Cl-C5 - classes of conditioning applied to common carrier lines in order to reduce errors and exceed normal amplitude and distortion specifications.

CLADDING - term used in fiber optics which refers to the glass that encircles the core fiber and acts like a mirror to reflect the light.

CLASS OF SERVICE (COS) - term used to describe a network connection by means of one of its variables, such as bandwidth or security.

CLEAR CHANNEL - transmission channel in which the total bandwidth is available for use.

CLEAR TO SEND (CTS) - term used in half-duplex modem communications which, in response to a Request-to-Send signal, indicates that data transmission may commence.

CLIENT/SERVER MODEL - any configuration which denotes one computer as a server, responding to requests for data or services, while another computer acts as a client requesting the data or services. In the OSI specifications, a client is referred to as the service requestor.

CLIPPING - refers to the trimming off or elimination of high and low frequencies which are greater than or less than the channel's bandwidth. Clipping may cause channel distortion.

CLNS - see *Connectionless Mode Network Service*.

CLOCKING - the generation of a regular signal which supplies a time basis for networking devices.

CLOSELY COUPLED NETWORKS - normally, channel-attached networks.

CLUSTER - a group of computers or terminals attached to a common controller.

CLUSTER CONTROLLER (CC) - any device which acts as a communications or I/O manager for a cluster.

CLUSTER TERMINAL CONTROLLER (CTC) - see *cluster controller*.

CMC - see *Communications Management Configuration*.

CMIP - see *Common Management Information Protocol*.

CMIPDU - see *Common Management Information Protocol Data Unit*.

CMIPM - see *Common Management Information Protocol Machine*.

CMIS - see *Common Management Information Service*.

CMISE - see *Common Management Information Service Element*.

CMOL - see *Common Management Information Protocol over Logical Link Control*.

CMOT - see *Common Management Information Protocol over the Transmission Control Protocol.*

CMS - see *Conversational Monitor System.*

CNR - see *Carrier-to-Noise Ratio.*

CO - see *Central Office.*

CO-CHANNEL INTERFERENCE - interference created by the transmission of signals in opposite directions via adjacent lines.

COAXIAL CABLE - cable used for data transmission; consists of an unbalanced pair of wires made up of an inner conductor encompassed by a grounded, braided or solid conductor.

CODE PAGE - an IBM term which describes IBM's specific assignment of graphic characters and control functions to all code points contained in a code set.

CODE SET - refers to all the possible values of a code.

CODER - a device used to convert analog signals to digital signals.

CODING - any scheme which alters the portrayal of data from one form to another. Analog-to-digital conversion is an example of coding.

COLLISION - as used in communications, the act of two or more network devices transmitting at the same time on the same transmission channel.

COLLISION AVOIDANCE - see *CSMA/CA.*

COMBINED STATION - in an unbalanced network, any station capable of being both a transmitting and a receiving station.

COMMON APPLICATION SERVICE ELEMENT (CASE) - refers to application-level common service elements (such as recovery and logging) of the OSI reference model.

COMMON CARRIER - term used to refer to private telecommunications companies.

COMMON COMMUNICATIONS SUPPORT - an IBM term referring to the SAA interface which defines the data formats and protocols available in an SAA environment.

COMMON MANAGEMENT INFORMATION PROTOCOL (CMIP) - protocol used in the OSI reference model for management information exchange between application layers.

COMMON MANAGEMENT INFORMATION PROTOCOL DATA UNIT (CMIPDU) - refers to a data structure used in CMIP.

COMMON MANAGEMENT INFORMATION PROTOCOL MACHINE (CMIPM) - refers to any network entity which services CMIP.

COMMON MANAGEMENT INFORMATION PROTOCOL OVER LOGICAL LINK CONTROL (CMOL) - network management scheme to manage devices on a mixed-media LAN.

COMMON MANAGEMENT INFORMATION PROTOCOL OVER THE TRANSMISSION CONTROL PROTOCOL (CMOT) - dual protocol approach for the simultaneous running of SNMP and CMIP.

COMMON MANAGEMENT INFORMATION SERVICE (CMIS) - service used in the OSI reference model for communications system management.

COMMON MANAGEMENT INFORMATION SERVICE ELEMENT (CMISE) - management information service object within the OSI reference model.

COMMON PROGRAMMING INTERFACE - an IBM term referring to an SAA interface which defines routines for accessing files, programs and communications devices in an SAA application.

COMMON SERVICE APPLICATION ELEMENT (CSAE) - term used by the ISO in describing specific functions within the application layer.

COMMON USER ACCESS (CUA) - an IBM term referring to the IBM standard for data display within SAA.

COMMON USER INTERFACE - an IBM term used in SAA applications defining the characteristics of text and graphics screens by SAA-compliant programs in an SAA application.

COMMUNICATIONS ADAPTER - any device used to connect a computer to a communications facility.

COMMUNICATIONS CONTROL CHARACTERS - see *control characters*.

COMMUNICATIONS CONTROLLER - device for the management of communications lines between a computer and other devices.

COMMUNICATIONS CONTROLLER NODE - an IBM phrase used as a general term to describe physical units which conform to SNA Physical Unit Type 4 specifications.

COMMUNICATIONS INTERFACE UNIT (CIU) - refers to the actual physical mechanism or device (such as a telephone) which permits ingress to a communications facility.

COMMUNICATIONS LINE TRANSMISSION MODE - refers to the communications technique being used on a line, such as simplex, half-duplex and full-duplex.

COMMUNICATIONS LINKS SNA - an IBM term referring to the path messages travel between nodes in an SNA network.

COMMUNICATIONS MANAGEMENT CONFIGURATION (CMC) - refers to the required network management protocols and procedures and how they are configured.

COMMUTATOR - as defined for telecommunications, the hardware which permits the attachment of input channels to a multiplexer.

COMPANDING - the process of compressing speech upon transmission (and decompressing it at reception) to allow for better utilization of the available transmission bandwidth. *Compand* is a contraction of the words "compress" and "expand".

COMPLETION CODE - the final result value returned by an adapter after servicing a request.

COMPOSITE LINK - a communications channel which carries multiplexed data.

COMPRESSION - the reduction of the number of bits required to define the transmitted data.

COMPUTER-AIDED NETWORK MANAGEMENT (CANM) - refers to a software system for the automated or semi-automated management of a communications network.

COMPUTER-BASED MESSAGE SYSTEM (CBMS) - see *electronic mail.*

COMPUTERIZED BRANCH EXCHANGE (CBX) - refers to a computer-controlled PBX.

CONCATENATION - refers to the method of connecting multiple point-to-point circuits into a single end-to-end connection.

CONCENTRATION - the process of receiving messages from multiple lines and then retransmitting them onto fewer outgoing lines.

CONCENTRATOR - a device which performs concentration; similar in concept to a multiplexer, but containing memory for the storing of messages before retransmission.

CONDITIONING - the treatment of leased lines by common carriers in order to improve line performance and reduce errors.

CONDUCTED MEDIA - any media which utilizes a conductor of some type for transmission.

CONFIGURATION - see *network architecture*.

CONFIGURATION CONTROL - the documentation used to describe a network and its associated policies and procedures.

CONFIGURATION MANAGEMENT - refers to the methodology used for the management of resources within a network.

CONFORMANCE - a measure of the performance of network components (including policies and procedures) against their rated specifications.

CONGESTION - network condition which results when more traffic is being placed on the network than it can reasonably handle.

CONGESTION CONTROL - any scheme for the reduction of delays and blockages on a network.

CONNECTION CONTROL - any mechanism for the creation and management of a connection between two network nodes.

CONNECTION ESTABLISHMENT - either a virtual or direct physical circuit and its associated procedures whereby a requesting station establishes contact with another station.

CONNECTION POINT MANAGER (CPMGR) - any protocol object charged with establishing and managing connection requests.

CONNECTION-ORIENTED DATA TRANSFER - any protocol in which virtual circuits are used for data exchange.

CONNECTIONLESS DATA TRANSFER - any methodology for data transfer (acknowledged or unacknowledged) which doesn't use virtual circuits.

CONNECTIONLESS MODE NETWORK SERVICE (CLNS) - transport layer data transfer utility which uses connectionless data transfer methods.

CONNECTIVITY - refers to the degree to which network devices may be connected.

CONSTANT RATIO CODE - coding scheme in which all code points have the same ratio of 1's to 0's.

CONSTANT VALUE LOGS - the network flat loss caused by passive devices.

CONSULTATIVE COMMITTEE ON INTERNATIONAL TELEPHONE AND TELEGRAPH (CCITT) - international standards group on telecommunications.

CONTENT SYNCHRONIZATION - refers to the requirement of some networks that message frames be delivered in the exact sequence transmitted.

CONTENTION - method of access to a network medium in which the first device to obtain access to a channel has control and in which conflicts between devices are settled via a resolution methodology.

CONTENTION BUS - any bus-oriented network which utilizes contention techniques for access to the bus.

CONTEXT DATA - presentation-layer data used to warrant that the negotiation-phase syntax and semantics are used throughout data transfer.

CONTEXT SET - term used in the OSI reference model to indicate the results of the negotiations phase at the presentation layer of the model.

CONTEXT-DEPENDENT CODING - data-coding scheme in which the generated code is based upon previously transmitted data.

CONTINUOUS ARQ - type of error-detection scheme in which data is sent on one channel, and ACKS and NACKS are sent over a reverse channel.

CONTINUOUS CARRIER - any transmission system in which a carrier wave is always present on the line.

CONTINUOUS RQ - error-control methodology used at the data-link layer which uses the retransmission of data frames in error, without doing so in a stop-and-wait manner.

CONTINUOUS SIGNAL - a signal, such as a sine wave, which is capable of assuming all values within a given interval.

CONTINUOUSLY VARIABLE SLOPE DELTA MODULATION (CVSD) - analog voice signal-to-digital signal encoding scheme.

CONTROL BITS - bits which provide interface device control over signals.

CONTROL BYTE - any specific pattern of bits whose charter is to initiate, terminate or modify a control activity.

CONTROL CHARACTERS - multiple control bytes.

CONTROL FIELD - an 8- or 16-bit field used in HDLC or SDLC frames to define the frame type and to control frame sequencing.

CONTROL TOKEN - specific bit pattern used in token-passing networks which gives a network node permission to transmit data.

CONTROL UNIT TERMINAL (CUT) - an IBM term for general-purpose workstations.

CONVERSATIONAL MODE - operational technique in which entries and their associated responses occur in an alternating pattern between two devices or between a device and a user.

CONVERSATIONAL MONITOR SYSTEM (CMS) - an IBM term which describes the mainframe-based interface between users and the Control Program (CP) of IBM's VM operating system.

CONVERTER - any hardware or software device designed for the transformation of information from one form to another.

CONVOLUTION - data-coding scheme in which a device's memory is used to store output bit sequences because of their dependence upon previous input bit sequences.

CORE GATEWAY - an Internet Network Operations Center-operated router which distributes reachability information between the autonomous systems attaching to the Internet backbone circuits.

COS - see *Class of Service*.

COSINE WAVE - the representation of a wave after the cosine function is applied to angles between 0 and 360 degrees.

CPMGR - see *Connection Point Manager*.

CPS - see *characters per second*.

CRC - see *Cyclic Redundancy Check*.

CREDIT ALLOCATION SCHEME - term used within the OSI reference model for flow control at the transport layer. A sliding window protocol is used for flow control via a credit value (in the credit field of the frame) which allocates a fixed number of buffers for a connection and reduces this number every time a Transport Protocol Data Unit (TPDU) is received.

CROSSBAR SWITCH - type of matrix switch used in early circuit-switching equipment.

CROSSTALK - type of signal noise created by the transmission of signals from an adjacent or nearby channel.

CSAE - see *Common Service Application Element*.

CSDN - see *Circuit-Switched Data Network*.

CSMA - see *Carrier Sense Multiple Access*.

CSMA/CA - see *Carrier Sense Multiple Access with Collision Avoidance*.

CSMA/CAPA - see *Carrier Sense Multiple Access with Collision Avoidance and Positive Acknowledgment*.

CSMA/CD - see *Carrier Sense Multiple Access with Collision Detection*.

CSMA/CP - see *Carrier Sense Multiple Access with Collision Prevention*.

CST - see *Channel Slot Time.*

CSU - see *Channel Service Unit.*

CTC - see *Cluster Terminal Controller.*

CTS - see *Clear to Send* and *Customer Test Service.*

CUA - see *Common User Access.*

CURRENT - as measured in amperes (amps), a measure of the number of electrons (electrical charge) moving past a specific point in a given unit of time.

CURRENT LOOP - interface between a device and a circuit in which 0's and 1's are used to denote the presence or absence of current (or some other signal).

CUSTOMER INFORMATION CONTROL SYSTEM (CICS) - an IBM term used to describe the communications monitoring software which performs interface functions between the operating system, applications programming, file access requests and communications access, in addition to running line handling, contention recovery work scheduling, recovery from communications failure, system recovery and administrative duties. Recently announced for PCs and the AS/400.

CUSTOMER TEST SERVICE (CTS) - form of digital loopback test used with DSU/CSU equipment.

CUT - see *Control Unit Terminal.*

CVSD - see *Continuously Variable Slope Delta Modulation.*

CWM - see *Carrier Wave Modulation.*

CYCLIC REDUNDANCY CHECK (CRC) - error-detection scheme in which a multibit sum is appended to the end of a transmission block. This sum is created from cyclically weighted values, each of which is added to the sum, via binary addition with no carry, if it corresponds to the occurence of a 1 bit. The receiver goes through the same process and then compares the results. If equal, no error has occurred. Typical forms of the CRC are: CRC-12 (12-bit sum), CRC-16 (16-bit sum) and CRC-32 (32-bit sum).

D

D CHANNEL - an ISDN term referring to a channel used to transmit control information.

D CONNECTOR - EIA standard connectors, such as the RS-232, which resemble the letter "D". D connectors come in may different sizes and wiring configurations.

D/A - see *Digital-to-Analog Converter.*

D/I - see *Drop and Insert.*

DAA - see *Data Access Arrangement.*

DAISY CHAINING - a method of connecting network devices in series, also known as *cascading*.

DAL - see *Data Access Language.*

DAMA - see *Demand Assignment Multiple Access.*

DAP - see *Directory Access Protocol.*

DAS - see *Dual-Attached Station.*

DATA - a symbolic representation of an idea or measurement.

DATA ACCESS ARRANGEMENT (DAA) - FCC-mandated device when user's hardware is not FCC-certified for use with the public telephone network.

DATA ACCESS LANGUAGE (DAL) - a standard used by Apple Computer Corporation to access heterogeneous server databases from a Macintosh client, including the AS/400 relational database.

DATA CIRCUIT EQUIPMENT (DCE) - hardware designed to terminate a data communications circuit; modems, for example.

DATA CIRCUIT TRANSPARENCY - refers to a circuit designed to transmit all data without alteration to its contents.

DATA CODE - any bit pattern used to symbolize data.

DATA COLLECTION - the automatic sensing, acquiring and storage of data.

DATA COMMUNICATIONS - the transmission via electronic means over communications links of binary or character data.

DATA COMPRESSION - as defined for telecommunications, the changing of the logical form of data so that it takes less time to transmit.

DATA CONCENTRATION - refers to the use of a single communications link to transmit data from multiple links.

DATA DIRECTORY - list of all stored network data.

DATA DISTRIBUTION SYSTEM - any network design scheme in which data is sent from a central site to remote sites on demand.

DATA ENCODING - refers to representing of a data value with a signal value.

DATA ENCRYPTION STANDARD (DES) - NIST-endorsed data encryption and decryption standard.

DATA FLOW CONTROL IN SNA - IBM term referring to the data flow control layer of the company's SNA product which is charged with session integrity between NAUs.

DATA LINK - generic term referring to the transmission medium and related hardware required to establish a data communications link between a source and a destination.

DATA LINK CONFIGURATION - generic term referring to the topology of a data communications link.

DATA LINK CONTROL (DLC) - refers to the set of control operations required for a communications link.

DATA LINK ESCAPE (DLE) - bisync control character used to realize data transparency.

DATA LINK LAYER - OSI reference model term which refers to the second layer which is charged with setting up and managing a communications link.

DATA LINK PROCESSOR (DLP) - a control unit used to connect multiple devices to a computer.

DATA LINK PROTOCOL DATA UNIT (DPDU) - OSI term that refers to the form in which data is formatted for use by the data-link control layer of an OSI network.

DATA LINK PROTOCOLS - generic term for those protocols which set up and manage a communications link.

DATA LINK RELAY - a bridge.

DATA MESSAGE - data link protocol message which differs from the standard by containing data as well as control information.

DATA NETWORK IDENTIFICATION CODE (DNIC) - term used to refer to the four-digit code attribute of a public network. This code also gives an indication as to the services which are available with the network.

DATA OVER VOICE PROCESSING - transmission scheme which allows for both data and voice to be sent over the same channel.

DATA OVERRUN - transmission error condition in which the transmitted data exceeds the memory buffer assigned for its storage.

DATA RATE - measurement of transmission speed, normally in bits per second (bps).

DATA SERVICE UNIT (DSU) - a device designed to interface between digital telephone lines and data terminal equipment.

DATA SET - generic name for a modem.

DATA SET CHANGE - communications interface control signal reflecting a change in either the carrier, the CTS signal or the DTR signal.

DATA SET CLOCKING - clock-based signaling scheme which modems use to control transmissions.

DATA SET READY (DSR) - modem control signal marking its powered-up, ready state.

DATA SHARING - network facility for allowing nodes to access data stored at a different node.

DATA SINK - the DTE which is the destination for a transmission.

DATA SOURCE - the point of origin for a transmission.

DATA STREAM - data flowing from one network node to another.

DATA STREAMING - high-speed transmission protocol in which the transmitting device stays in a transmission mode for extended periods of time.

DATA SWITCH - refers to a line-switching device used to switch data (nonvoice) lines.

DATA TERMINAL EQUIPMENT (DTE) - devices connected to a network whose function is to send and receive data.

DATA TERMINAL READY (DTR) - signal sent from DTE to DCE indicating ready-to-proceed status.

DATA TRANSFER PHASE - refers to that stage of a data link protocol during which packets of data are sent from one node to another.

DATA TRANSFER RATE - see *data rate*.

DATA TRANSMISSION - generic term for the sending of data from one point to another.

DATA TRANSMISSION INTERFACE - a shared boundary defined by a common set of functional characteristics.

DATA TRANSPARENCY - data link control facility which allows characters to be placed within the information field of a frame without having them treated as control characters.

DATA UNIT (DU) - OSI reference model term used to denote an FTAM application data unit.

DATA-SWITCHING EXCHANGE (DSE) - a generic term for a switching or routing digital network node.

DATABASE DUPLICATION - refers to the process of copying a database at nodes within a network, thus distributing the database.

DATAGRAM - 1) a packet in a datagram service-oriented packet-switching network; 2) a packet-switching service which independently routes packets between source and destination without assuring sequenced delivery of the packets. Packets may, in fact, be discarded under special circumstances.

DATAGRAM LIFETIME - refers to the amount of time required from generation until delivery of a datagram.

DATAPHONE DIGITAL SERVICE (DDS) - AT&T's digital communications service.

db - see *Decibel*.

dbmV - see *Decibel-Millivolt*.

dbW - see *Decibel-Watt*.

DBX - see *Digital PBX*.

DC - see *Direct Current*.

DCA - see *Document Content Architecture*.

DCE - see *Data Circuit Equipment*.

DDI - see *Digital Data Interface*.

DDM - see *Distributed Data Management*.

DDS - see *Dataphone Digital Service*.

DEADLOCK - network condition in which two devices are in a wait mode, pending transmission from the other. Deadlocks require some sort of meddling for resolution.

DECIBEL (db) - the measure of the power of a signal relative to a second signal, which describes attenuation.

DECIBEL-MILLIVOLT (dbmV) - decibel measure in which the input voltage is constant at 1 millivolt.

DECIBEL-WATT (dbW) - decibel measure in which the input power is constant at 1 watt.

DECODER - generic term for a device which converts digital signals to analog signals.

DECOMPRESSION - refers to the process of restoring compressed data back into its original, uncompressed state.

DEGRADATION - a loss of peak performance in a network.

DELAY - time between an action and its effect.

DELAY DISTORTION - also called envelope delay, this type of signal distortion is caused by a difference in speed of the component signals in a complex waveform.

DELAY EQUALIZER - device designed to add delay to an analog signal in order to eliminate delay distortion.

DELIMITER - a bit pattern which defines the limits of a message, a token or a frame.

DELINEATION OF DATA - refers to the use of special character or bit groupings to mark the beginning or ending of message data.

DELTA MODULATION (DM) - modulation scheme in which the digitizing of an analog signal is acccomplished by comparing two samples of the signal. The DM scheme involves assigning a 1 bit if the second sample is greater in value than the first, and a 0 bit if it isn't.

DELTA ROUTING - routing scheme combining fixed and distributed adaptive routings.

DEMAND ASSIGNMENT MULTIPLE ACCESS (DAMA) - channel allocation scheme for satellites which employs either TDM or FDM modulation schemes.

DEMARCATION POINT - an AT&T term used to define the point at which the public telephone network begins and a customer's premises ends.

DEMODULATOR - device which extracts the modulated signal from a modulated carrier.

DEMULTIPLEXER - device which extracts the component signals from a multiplexed signal.

DES - see *Data Encryption Standard.*

DESIGNATED BRIDGE - network device which only performs bridging functions in a LAN.

DESTINATION - the physical device which is the destination, and therefore the end, of a transmission.

DESTINATION ADDRESS - the network address of a destination.

DESTINATION FIELD - that portion of a transmission frame which contains the destination address.

DESTINATION SERVICE ACCESS POINT (DSAP) - refers to the service access point of a destination node in Ethernet's logical link control.

DETECTION - any scheme by which a receiver identifies a signal.

DETERMINISTIC CSMA/CD - variation of the CSMA/CD protocol which uses deterministic processes to handle high traffic loads.

DEVICE BUFFER - an IBM term for the area in memory of a terminal or printer, in which data is stored before being displayed.

DEVICE CONTROL CHARACTERS - any control character used to turn transmission equipment on or off.

DFS - see *Distributed File Service* and *Distributed File System*.

DFT - see *Distributed Function Terminal*.

DIA - see *Document Interchange Architecture*.

DIAL-UP BACKUP - using two dial-up lines as a recovery mechanism for a failed dedicated, full-duplex line.

DIAL-UP LINE - any data circuit accessed by means of a dialing procedure. Opposite of a leased line.

DIALOGUE - any two-way process of system and user interaction.

DIBITS - transmission scheme in which two bits of data are combined into one signal.

DIFFERENTIAL CODING - signal-coding scheme which utilizes the differences between successive signals.

DIFFERENTIAL MANCHESTER ENCODING - signal-encoding scheme in which signal polarity is determined by the last half of the previously transmitted bit cell. To signal a 1, the preceding signal element would be the same polarity as the first half of the current bit cell; a 0 would result if the preceding signal polarity is opposite.

DIFFERENTIAL PHASE SHIFT KEYING (DPSK) - phase modulation scheme in which the phase of a cycle in the current time period is contrasted to the phase in a previous period to determine 1's and 0's.

DIFFERENTIAL PULSE-CODED MODULATION - pulse-coded modulation scheme in which binary signals are used to represent the differences between consecutive signal samples.

DIGITAL CIRCUIT - any circuit which represents data by means of pulsed digital signals.

DIGITAL COMMUNICATIONS CHANNEL - any communications channel specifically designed to transmit and receive digital signals.

DIGITAL DATA - any data that consists of discrete values such as binary 1's and 0's.

DIGITAL DATA INTERFACE (DDI) - refers to any adapter or other device that attaches to fiber-optic cables or shielded twisted-pair cables using the FDDI/SDDI standards.

DIGITAL DATA SWITCH - any switching device capable of manipulating digital signals.

DIGITAL LINE TERMINATION - the point at which a digital circuit connects to a line-terminating device.

DIGITAL MODEM - digital device which combines the functions of a DSU and a CSU into one unit.

DIGITAL MULTIPLEXED INTERFACE (DMI) - the point of interface at which several digital signals become multiplexed onto a digital circuit.

DIGITAL PBX (DBX) - digital network-switching device for private networks used to combine a digital LAN with a digital voice network.

DIGITAL PHASE LOCKED LOOP (DPLL) - data-signal sampling circuit designed to sample signals at a rate higher than the signaling rate in order to acquire the signal element's beginning and end.

DIGITAL PIPE - see *digital circuit.*

DIGITAL REPEATERS - digital version of an analog signal repeater.

DIGITAL SERVICE UNIT (DSU) - line interface adapters used in digital data transmissions which ensure proper digital signal characteristics.

DIGITAL SHARING UNIT - any device created to permit the sharing of a single digital communications link by multiple devices.

DIGITAL SIGNAL - signaling scheme in which there are only a discrete number of states permitted so as to allow these states to represent digital data values.

DIGITAL SIGNAL PROCESSOR (DSP) - any device which is able to manipulate digital signals.

DIGITAL SPEECH INTERPOLATION (DSI) - digital multiplexing scheme in which voice signals are multiplexed and transmitted only when voice signals are present.

DIGITAL SWITCHING - switching scheme for digital signals which permits them to remain in digital form without having to be translated back into analog signals.

DIGITAL TERMINATION SERVICE - refers to the DSU/CSU service of terminating digital circuit.

DIGITAL-TO-ANALOG (D/A) CONVERTER - any device which is designed to convert digital signals into analog signals.

DIGITIZATION - the conversion of data from analog to digital signals.

DIGITIZER - any device capable of digitization.

DIPLEX - transmission scheme in which two signals are sent in opposite directions, normally at different frequencies, on a single circuit.

DIRECT CONNECT MODEMS - modems which have integrated modular jacks for plugging into the public telephone system without the need for a telephone set.

DIRECT CURRENT (DC) - a type of electrical current which maintains a constant and unchanging magnitude.

DIRECT STORE-AND-FORWARD DEADLOCK - form of deadlock found in store-and-forward networks which results from the lack of available buffers between the two deadlocked nodes.

DIRECTIONALITY - term used to refer to transmitting in one direction at a given frequency and receiving data on another frequency. Used in to/from head-end communications in broadband LANs.

DIRECTORY - a list of completely qualified network addresses and their associated network resources.

DIRECTORY ACCESS PROTOCOL (DAP) - protocol used by the directory user agent when accessing an X.500 directory.

DIRECTORY HASHING - Novell NetWare scheme in which the file server maps all directory files and retains this information in RAM.

DIRECTORY INFORMATION TREE (DIT) - generic term used to refer to the entire X.500 directory database.

DIRECTORY SERVICE (DS) - OSI term used to denote the translation from symbolic names into fully qualified network addresses.

DIRECTORY SYSTEM AGENTS (DSA) - generic term used to refer to the different databases which comprise the X.500 directory.

DIRECTORY USER AGENT (DUA) - that portion of an X.500 system which is used to access an X.500 directory.

DIS - see *Draft International Standards.*

DISC - see *Disconnect Command.*

DISCONNECT COMMAND (DISC) - HDLC-based command used to terminate a logical link.

DISCONNECTED MODE RESPONSE (DM) - HDLC-based command used to report the logical disconnection of a secondary station.

DISCRETE DATA - data, such as binary, which has a finite number of values.

DISCRETE SIGNAL - a signal with discrete (finite) values.

DISOSS - see *Distributed Office Support System.*

DISPERSION - term used in open-air transmissions which refers to the dissipation of signals due to interference with the Earth's atmosphere.

DISTINCTIVE SIGNALING - any signaling scheme which is capable of discriminating between classes of conditions.

DISTORTION - refers to any unwanted or undesirable alteration in the shape or timing of a signal during transmission.

DISTRIBUTED DATA MANAGEMENT (DDM) - IBM's term for its midrange-based software product which allows access to data files at remote locations across a network.

DISTRIBUTED FILE SERVICE (DFS) - an OSI file server technology.

DISTRIBUTED FILE SYSTEM (DFS) - concept in which files are scattered throughout a network but are available to application programs as if they were resident at the node requesting file access.

DISTRIBUTED FUNCTION TERMINAL (DFT) - an IBM term used in SNA to refer to a PC which acts as a LAN gateway.

DISTRIBUTED MANAGEMENT ENVIRONMENT (DME) - set of technologies for network and system management by the Open Software Foundation.

DISTRIBUTED NETWORK ARCHITECTURE - any network scheme in which no centralized network control mechanism is used.

DISTRIBUTED OFFICE SUPPORT SYSTEM (DISOSS) - an IBM term referring to one of its office support products. DISOSS includes functions for E-mail and document exchange.

DISTRIBUTED PROCESSING - network data-processing scheme in which a single transaction may be processed over multiple network nodes, or in which multiple equivalent transactions are dispersed for processing across multiple network nodes.

DISTRIBUTED RELATIONAL DATABASE ARCHITECTURE (DRDA) - an implementation of several lower-level architectures including Distributed Data Management, LU 6.2 and several other standards. It lets programmers implement distributed databases through a standard SQL interface.

DISTRIBUTION AMPLIFIER - RF signal amplifier used in broadband networks.

DISTRIBUTION PANEL - an IBM term used in token-ring networks to describe a rack-mounted patch panel.

DISTRIBUTIVE ROUTING - routing scheme in which independent routing selections are made by network nodes after consulting with neighboring nodes and the update of the routing table.

DIT - see *Directory Information Tree.*

DLC - see *Data Link Control.*

DLE - see *Data Link Escape.*

DLP - see *Data Link Processor.*

DM - see *Delta Modulation* and *Disconnected Mode response.*

DME - see *Distributed Management Environment.*

DMI - see *Digital Multiplexed Interface.*

DNIC - see *Data Network Identification Code.*

DNS - see *Domain Name System.*

DOCUMENT ARCHITECTURE - document model which contains its layout, content, and electronic transmission and storage instructions.

DOCUMENT CONTENT ARCHITECTURE (DCA) - an IBM term used to refer to the section of the IBM office automation model concerned with the content, structure and formatting of a document.

DOCUMENT INTERCHANGE ARCHITECTURE (DIA) - network office systems model concerned with everything from the creation to the transmission of complicated documents.

DOMAIN - an IBM term used in SNA to refer to all network resources under processor control. The grouping of resources under network management for management by a single object.

DOMAIN NAME SYSTEM (DNS) - refers to a group of distributed databases supplying information in a TCP/IP environment.

DOUBLE CURRENT - circuit design scheme in which no significance is attached to a zero-voltage condition.

DOUBLE SIDEBAND (DSB) - type of transmission in which both sidebands of a signal are transmitted.

DOUBLE SIDEBAND SUPPRESSED CARRIER (DSBSC) - type of transmission in which both sidebands of a signal are transmitted but not the carrier.

DOUBLE SIDEBAND TRANSMITTED CARRIER (DSBTC) - type of transmission in which both sidebands of a signal are transmitted along with the carrier.

DOWNLINK - satellite communications link which starts at the satellite and terminates at the appropriate earth station(s).

DOWNLOADING - the transferral of information from a central location to a remote location.

DOWNSTREAM - the direction of data flow in an IBM Token-Ring network.

DOWNTIME - time that a device is unavailable due to failure or malfunction.

DOWNWARD MULTIPLEXING - the inverse of normal multiplexing, downward multiplexing refers to the splitting of a single communications channel into a number of other channels.

DPDU - see *Data Link Protocol Data Unit.*

DPLL - see *Digital Phase Locked Loop.*

DPSK - see *Differential Phase Shift Keying.*

DRAFT INTERNATIONAL STANDARDS (DIS) - term which refers to the "draft" or preliminary version of a standard from one of the international standards organizations.

DRDA - see *Distributed Relational Database Architecture.*

DROP - any point at which a network device is attached to a transmission medium.

DROP AND INSERT (D/I) - refers to the process of demultiplexing a signal and then using the result as input to another multiplexer. Found in Tl transmissions.

DROP LINE - also called a drop cable, this is a cable which connects a network tap to a user's outlet.

DROP LINE DEVICE - as defined for use in broadband networks, any external device attached to coaxial cable via a drop line.

DROP OUT - the temporary loss of a signal caused by a transmission disturbance.

DS - see *Directory Service.*

DS-1 SIGNALING - PCM based data coding scheme in which an analog signal is sampled 8,000 times per second, yielding a gross transmission rate of 1.544mlbps.

DSA - see *Directory System Agents.*

DSAP - see *Destination Service Access Point.*

DSB - see *Double Sideband.*

DSBSC - see *Double Sideband Suppressed Carrier.*

DSBTC - see *Double Sideband Transmitted Carrier.*

DSE - see *Data-Switching Exchange.*

DSI - see *Digital Speech Interpolation.*

DSP - see *Digital Signal Processor.*

DSR - see *Data Set Ready.*

DSU - see *Data Service Unit* and *Digital Service Unit.*

DTE - see *Data Terminal Equipment.*

DTR - see *Data Terminal Ready.*

DU - see *Data Unit.*

DUA - see *Directory User Agent.*

DUAL ATTACHED STATION (DAS) - term used in FDDI which refers to the attachment of a single network station to the two fiber-optic rings outlined in the FDDI standard. The advantage to a DAS is that, if one ring fails, the station may continue to operate on the other ring.

DUAL CABLE - as defined for use in broadband networking, a type of LAN which incorporates two branching-tree networks, with each network sending signals in the opposite direction.

DUPLEX - see *full-duplex* or *half-duplex*.

DYNAMIC BANDWIDTH ALLOCATION - transmission scheme in which only devices that are transmitting are allocated channel space.

DYNAMIC CHANNEL ALLOCATION - any channel allocation scheme in which the capacity of a channel is allocated to multiple users based on demand.

DYNAMIC ROUTING - any routing scheme in which the route from source to destination for a transmitted message may vary during transmission.

E

E1 - a type of physical data link similar to T1.

EARTH STATION - refers to that section of a satellite communications system which is located on the earth and consists of an antenna complex and a transceiver or receiver.

EBCDIC - see *Extended Binary Coded Decimal Interchange Code.*

ECF - see *Enhanced Connectivity Feature.*

ECHO - the echoing or reflection of a transmitted signal due to the unmatched electrical characteristics of the connection between two devices or on a communications line.

ECHO CANCELLER - a device for eliminating echoes in transmitted communications. This is accomplished by creating a duplicate of the echo and then subtracting this duplicated image from the original echo, thereby eliminating it.

ECHO CHECK - refers to the transmission to the sender of echo images received to determine if the transmission was in error. If so, the original data is retransmitted; if not, no error occurred.

ECHOPLEX - a type of asynchronous communications protocol in which the receiver echoes or transmits back to the sender the characters that it has received.

EDAC - see *Error Detection and Correction.*

EDI - see *Electronic Data Interchange.*

EFFECTIVE BANDWIDTH - refers to that section of bandwidth used for transmission in which the greatest power is concentrated.

EFFECTIVE ISOTROPIC RADIATED POWER (EIRP) - normally stated in decibels (db), this is a rating of the amount of power received from a satellite at an earth station.

EFFECTIVE THROUGHPUT - a measurement of the actual number of bits transmitted during a given period of time. This measurement does not include error-checking or control bits or bits that were retransmitted due to a transmission error.

EFS - see *Error-Free Second.*

EGP - see *Exterior Gateway Protocol.*

EHLLAPI - see *Emulation High-Level Language Application Program Interface.*

EIA - see *Electronic Industries Association.*

EIRP - see *Effective Isotropic Radiated Power.*

EISA - see *Extended Industry Standard Architecture.*

ELECTROMAGNETIC INTERFERENCE - refers to the electrical "noise" in a circuit from the electromagnetic emissions of other circuits or devices.

ELECTRONIC BIT MAP - refers to an electronic image of a series of data bits.

ELECTRONIC DATA INTERCHANGE (EDI) - a group of services designed for document and information exchange. The emphasis of EDI is on eliminating the paper trail normally associated with everyday business transactions such as invoicing, purchase orders and other document-oriented transactions.

ELECTRONIC INDUSTRIES ASSOCIATION (EIA) - an organization established in North America for the purpose of establishing electronic and electrical standards and conventions.

ELECTRONIC MAIL - any network-based system for the storing and recalling of messages or other forms of data on a store-and-forward basis; also known as e-mail.

ELEMENT MANAGEMENT SYSTEMS (EMS) - refers to networking systems designed to support multiple network devices all supplied from a common manufacturer.

ELLC - see *Enhanced Logical Link Control.*

EMS - see *Element Management Systems.*

EMULATION HIGH-LEVEL LANGUAGE APPLICATION PROGRAM INTERFACE (EHLLAPI) - an IBM term referring to a set of application programs which utilize LU type 2 application program interfaces to interface with high-level languages such as Pascal, C and COBOL.

EMULATOR - any software, hardware or combination which copies or imitates the functions of some other device or system.

ENCAPSULATION - refers to the process of adding headers and/or trailers to a data stream, creating a data capsule, packet or message frame.

ENCODING - any strategy or technique used to represent transmitted data through the alteration of the transmitted signal.

ENCRYPTION - refers to the alteration of transmitted data into a form unprocessable except by the proposed receiver.

END NODE - any node in a network incapable of forwarding or rerouting data packets intended for delivery to other nodes in the network.

END OF BLOCK (EOB) - ASCII control character which denotes the end of a block of data.

END OF MESSAGE (EOM) - ASCII control character which denotes the end of a record or message.

END OF TEXT (ETX) - ASCII control character which denotes the completion or end of a transmission.

END OF TRANSMISSION BLOCK (ETB) - ASCII control character which denotes that a block check character is to follow; also indicates the end of a transmitted data block.

END-TO-END ROUTING - refers to any message-routing methodology in which the complete transmission route from source to destination is planned out before the message is transmitted.

ENDING DELIMITER - in an IBM Token-Ring environment, ending delimiter refers to a formatted byte used to specify the end of a token or frame.

ENHANCED CONNECTIVITY FEATURE (ECF) - an IBM term referring to a collection of micro-to-mainframe programs which allow for the sharing of printers, transfer of data files and the creation of virtual disks and virtual file servers. Using ECF, the host-based programs are referred to as servers and the PC-based programs are referred to as requestors.

ENHANCED LOGICAL LINK CONTROL (ELLC) - refers to an X.25 protocol which permits the transfer of data link control data between to adjacent SNA nodes connected via an X.25 link.

ENHANCED PERFORMANCE ARCHITECTURE (EPA) - refers to the local area network, real-time application subset of the Open Systems Architecture.

ENQ - see *Enquiry Character.*

ENQUIRY CHARACTER (ENQ) - ASCII control character which denotes the polling of a device.

ENTERPRISE NETWORKS - denoting any network designed to join all the computing resources in a company. Enterprise networks may join local area networks, wide area networks, file servers, mainframes and minicomputers among others.

ENTERPRISE SYSTEM CONNECTION ARCHITECTURE FACILITY (ESCAF) - an IBM term denoting the three-part host facility used with ES/9000 (System/390) series machines. The three parts are: a set of protocols for high-speed data transfer; fiber-optic channels for high-speed links between processors or processors and terminals; and high-speed, point-to-point, switched- line communications.

ENTRY POINT - any point in a network at which a device may join the network.

ENVELOPE - a term used in electrical signaling systems to denote the particular shape of a signal.

EOB - see *End of Block*.

EOM - see *End of Message*.

EPA - see *Enhanced Performance Architecture*.

EPP - see *Ethernet Packet Processor*.

EQUALIZER - any hardware device placed on a communications line to amend the line's frequency response characteristics.

ERROR - in data communications, an error occurs when the transmitted data does not match the data received.

ERROR DETECTION - refers to the process of being able to discern when a transmission error has occurred. Vertical Redundancy Check, Longitudinal Redundancy Check and block check characters are all forms of error detection.

ERROR DETECTION AND CORRECTION (EDAC) - an error-detection scheme in which the receiver is able to determine what the correct transmission should have been.

ERROR-FREE SECOND (EFS) - refers to the transmission of data for one second without error.

ESC - see *Escape*.

ESCAF - see *Enterprise System Connection Architecture Facility*.

ESCAPE (ESC) - ASCII control character denoting that an escape sequence will follow.

ESCAPE SEQUENCE - a group of control characters sent to indicate the beginning of a process or to set the status of a terminal.

ETB - see *End of Transmission Block*.

ETHERNET - Xerox Corporation's design, codified in the IEEE 802.3 specifications, for local area networks. Ethernet normally operates at 10Mbps, utilizing CSMA/CD for media access control.

ETHERNET PACKET PROCESSOR (EPP) - refers to any device capable of processing Ethernet message packets.

ETX - see *End of Text*.

EVEN PARITY - error-checking scheme in which all of the characters transmitted are forced to have an even numeric value.

EXCHANGE IDENTIFIER (XID) - a character string which indicates the specific central office-controlled exchange to which a given telephone is connected.

EXPLICIT RESERVATION - frequency reservation technique used in satellite systems. The reservation of a specific slot on a communications channel is called explicit.

EXPLICIT ROUTE - an IBM term used in SNA to indicate the section of a communications path which is in between originating and receiving subarea nodes.

EXTENDED BINARY CODED DECIMAL INTERCHANGE CODE (EBCDIC) - an IBM term referring to the eight-bit code for the representation of 256 different characters, numbers and symbols.

EXTENDED INDUSTRY STANDARD ARCHITECTURE (EISA) - 32-bit hardware bus compatible with 8- and 16-bit bus architectures.

EXTERIOR GATEWAY PROTOCOL (EGP) - a communications protocol developed to permit the sharing of information between autonomous systems.

EXTERNAL MODEM - any self-contained modem which resides outside of a computer and connects to the computer via a cable.

F

F BIT - as used in the SDLC protocol, this bit is the fifth in the control field. This bit is set to an "on" state by a secondary station in order to indicate the final frame of a transmission.

F CONNECTOR - as defined for use in broadband networking, a 75-ohm connector used to attach coaxial cables to equipment.

FACEPLATE - a plate for the connection of telephone and network connectors.

FACILITY BYPASS - any scheme of communications which sidesteps a network communications node but continues to supply the required network connectivity.

FADU - see *File Access Data Unit*.

FAIRNESS DOCTRINE - a fundamental principle of network routing design that has as its main precept the idea that all requests for service within a priority class should be treated fairly or equally.

FAN OUT - refers to a condition in which the number of input ports or lines is less than the number of output ports or lines.

FAST PACKET-SWITCHING - fixed-length packets are switched faster than variable-length packets in this packet-switching scheme.

FAST SELECT - refers to any transmission technique which sends data combined with the select request and doesn't differentiate between the select request, acknowledgment and the actual data transfer.

FAST-PACKET MULTIPLEXING (FPM) - version of time-division multiplexing which can give priority to a particular channel over the other channels being multiplexed.

FASTCONNECT CIRCUIT SWITCHING - the physical connection of two stations by means of an electronic switching mechanism.

FASTPATH - a type of high-speed gateway which connects AppleTalk and Ethernet networks.

FAULT MANAGEMENT - the process of managing network faults or failures in a controlled manner.

FAULT-TOLERANT - any system which has redundant components designed into it in order to allow the system to continue to function should a component fail.

FCS - see *Frame Check Sequence* and *Fiber Channel Standard*.

FDDI - see *Fiber Distributed Data Interface*.

FDM - see *Frequency-Division Multiplexing*.

FDMA - see *Frequency-Division Multiple Access*.

FDX - see *Full-Duplex*.

FEC - see *Forward Error Correction*.

FEDERAL INFORMATION PROCESSING STANDARDS (FIPS) - those standards which are issued by the National Institute for Standards and Technology (NIST).

FEDERAL TELECOMMUNICATIONS SYSTEM (FTS) - a network of leased lines used by the U.S. government to allow its employees to make telephone calls within the United States. The lines are leased from common carriers such as AT&T and US Sprint.

FEED - normally used with satellite or microwave systems, this is a transmission circuit which sends data to a high-speed backbone system.

FEP - see *Front-End Processor*.

FF - see *Form Feed*.

FIBER CHANNEL STANDARD (FCS) - refers to the specifications and standards for optical fiber channels used in conjunction with FDDI.

FIBER DISTRIBUTED DATA INTERFACE (FDDI) - standard specifications for a 100Mbps token-ring LAN using optical fiber to connect the nodes.

FIBER LOSS - a measure of the amount of energy loss of a light signal due to its transmission across a fiber-optic circuit.

FIBER-OPTIC CABLE - any cable which carries modulated light frequency signals. Normally made of glass, quartz or some other transparent material.

FIBER-OPTIC CIRCUITS - any circuit which uses fiber-optic cable as its transmission medium.

FIBER-OPTIC INTERREPEATER LINK (FIRL) - fiber-optic linkage between two networks incorporating a repeater on each of the networks.

FIFO - see *First-In, First-Out*.

FILE ACCESS DATA UNIT (FADU) - refers to the access to the subtree of a network node which represents a portion of a virtual file store, as used in FTAM applications.

FILE SEPARATOR (FS) - any control character used to indicate the end of a particular file.

FILE SERVER - a network device which processes the filing requests of other network nodes.

FILE TRANSFER AND ACCESS METHOD (FTAM) - refers to a set of specifications for access to and/or transferral of remote files between systems as defined by the OSI.

FILE TRANSFER METHOD (FTM) - see *File Transfer and Access Method*.

FILE TRANSFER PROTOCOL (FTP) - refers to a TCP service which enables management of file transfers across a network.

FILE TRANSFER SERVICE (FTS) - any network service whose task is to transfer files between stations.

FILTER - any device whose task is to remove frequencies from a transmitted signal.

FIPS - see *Federal Information Processing Standards*.

FIRL - see *Fiber optic Interrepeater Link*.

FIRST-IN, FIRST-OUT (FIFO) - queuing management scheme in which the first queue entry received is the first to be processed.

FIRST-LEVEL INTERRUPT HANDLER (FLIH) - any interrupt-handling scheme in which a first interrupt handler is charged with determining where the interrupt being processed came from, and a second interrupt handler is charged with processing the interrupt request.

FIXED ROUTING - the opposite of dynamic routing, fixed routing assumes that the routes between all possible pairs of network nodes are predetermined.

FLAG - a bit or bits used to signify special conditions or to trigger special actions.

FLAG FIELD - an eight-bit value (01111110) used in SDLC and HDLC protocols to indicate both the start and the end of a field.

FLAT LOSS - refers to an equal loss of signal power across network's entire bandwidth.

FLAT NAMING - any network entity naming methodology in which names are assigned to entities in such a way as to have no relationship to any other entity name.

FLIH - see *First-Level Interrupt Handler*.

FLOODING - packet-switched routing scheme in which identical packets are sent to every network destination as a means of ensuring that the intended target site receives the message.

FLOW CONTROL - any process which controls the flow of information within a network.

FM - see *Frequency Modulation.*

FMDS - see *Function Management Data Services.*

FOCAL POINT - the host computer on an IBM network.

FORM FEED (FF) - any control character used to signal a printer to advance the form by one page.

FORMAT - refers to the order in which data is arranged so that it may be processed in a controlled and predetermined manner.

FORMAT EFFECTORS - any communications control character providing formatted data in a stream.

FORWARD BANDPASS - that band of frequencies which is used in broadband systems to transmit outgoing signals from attached devices.

FORWARD CHANNEL - that channel allocated to carry information from the caller to the called destination.

FORWARD ERROR CORRECTION (FEC) - the process of adding bits to a transmitted character so that the receiver may detect and correct any transmission errors.

FOUR-WIRE CIRCUIT - wiring scheme using four transmission wires, two in each direction.

FPM - see *Fast-Packet Multiplexing.*

FRACTIONAL T3 - a service similar to fractional T1, except that a 44.7364Mbps T3 line is "fractionated" to allow T1 and/or T2 usage.

FRACTIONAL T1 - a service in which customers purchase a portion or "fraction" of a T1 circuit. The fractions are normally 128, 256, 384 or 512Kbps in size.

FRAGMENTATION - the process of breaking up a TCP/IP datagram into smaller pieces.

FRAME - that entity, defined by the data-link layer protocol, which is transmitted from source to receiver; e.g., an SDLC frame.

FRAME CHECK SEQUENCE (FCS) - error-checking scheme using multibit codes attached to the end of a transmission frame.

FRAME REJECT RESPONSE (FRMR) - response from a secondary SDLC station which has received an invalid frame.

FRAME RELAY - a form of packet-switching in which data frames are relayed to their destination with no attempt at error resolution made by the intermediate nodes. If an error occurs, retransmission must be end-to-end.

FRAME STATUS - an IBM term used with IBM Token-Ring networks to describe a frame byte which trails the ending delimiter byte and to specify whether or not the destination adapter received the transmitted frame.

FRAME SYNCHRONIZATION - any scheme which guarantees that a receiver is able to decode bit patterns sent to it.

FRAMING - refers to the process of placing control characters on either side of a data frame or block before transmission occurs.

FRAMING BIT - start/stop bits which frame asynchronous transmissions.

FREQUENCY - the rate at which a signal pattern is repeated; measured in Hertz. The rate of oscillation of a sine wave.

FREQUENCY AGILE MODEM - refers to modems which have the ability to search an assigned band of frequencies in order to locate an available frequency.

FREQUENCY CONVERTER - any device whose job is to convert an incoming frequency to another outgoing frequency.

FREQUENCY HOPPING - refers to any process in which multiple communications channels on multiple frequencies are used for the same data transmission.

FREQUENCY MODULATION (FM) - the process of varying the frequency of an analog signal to carry digital data.

FREQUENCY OFFSET - a type of signal distortion which causes a change in the frequency of a received signal.

FREQUENCY RESPONSE - refers to the band of frequencies which may be transmitted without distortion.

FREQUENCY SHIFT KEYING (FSK) - asynchronous modem modulation technique in which one frequency is used to represent 1's and another frequency is used to indicate 0's.

FREQUENCY-DIVISION MULTIPLE ACCESS (FDMA) - scheme for providing several access paths to a communications entity through the division of the access bandwidth into several individual channels.

FREQUENCY-DIVISION MULTIPLEXING (FDM) - multiplexing scheme in which multiple low-speed devices share a single transmission line by occupying different analog transmission frequencies.

FRMR - see *Frame Reject response.*

FRONT-END PROCESSOR (FEP) - any device located between a network and a host computer whose job is to control or manage communications.

FS - see *File Separator.*

FSK - see *Frequency Shift Keying.*

FTAM - see *File Transfer and Access Method.*

FTM - see *File Transfer Method.*

FTP - see *File Transfer Protocol.*

FTS - see *Federal Telecommunications System* and *File Transfer Service*

FULL-DUPLEX (FDX) - data communications mode in which transmission occurs in both directions at the same time.

FULLY CONNECTED NETWORK - a network design scheme in which every network node is connected to every other network node.

FUNCTION BASE - an IBM term used to designate the basic (without additional features or options) of a given machine.

FUNCTION MANAGEMENT DATA SERVICES (FMDS) - an IBM term referring to a sublayer of the SNA function management layer whose task is the presentation of data and the control of network activities for the network users.

FUNCTIONAL LAYERS - a generic term referring to the layers in a system's architecture. The OSI model, for example, has seven functional layers.

G

GAIN HIT - type of signal distortion distinguished by a limited duration increase in signal amplitude.

GATEWAY - describes any device joining two networks of dissimilar protocols and performing the required protocol conversion between them.

GATEWAY-TO-GATEWAY PROTOCOL (GGP) - an Internet term describing a formerly used protocol designed for the exchange of routing information between core routers.

GCS - see *Group Control System.*

GDMO - see *Guidelines for the Definition of Managed Objects.*

GENERAL FORMAT IDENTIFIER (GFI) - term used in packet-switching networks to describe the first field in a packet. Defined in the X.25 standard.

GENERATOR POLYNOMIAL - refers to the description of a specific bit pattern via polynomial expression, used in the detection and correction of data errors.

GEOSYNCHRONOUS SATELLITE - a satellite in a fixed orbit around the earth at an altitude of approximately 22,300 miles. Such a satellite has an orbital period the same as the earth and thus will appear to be stationary with respect to a point on earth directly beneath the satellite.

GFI - see *General Format Identifier.*

GGP - see *Gateway-to-Gateway Protocol.*

GHz - see *GigaHertz.*

GIGAHERTZ (GHz) - one billion cycles per second.

GLOBAL NAME - a name that all segments of a network know, as compared to a local name known only to one segment.

GLOBAL QUEUE - a queue known to all segments of a network, as compared to a local queue which is known to only one segment.

GO-BACK-N ARQ - a communications request issued by a receiver composed of a negative response to the receipt of a message in error, and the subsequent ignoring of any other messages until the message in error is received correctly.

GOSIP - see *Government OSI profile.*

GOVERNMENT OSI PROFILE (GOSIP) - a subset of the OSI reference model standards designed for use by government projects.

GRADED INDEX - a type of optical fiber with fused-together core and cladding to allow the index of refraction to change gradually from core to cladding.

GROUP ADDRESS - a network address shared by a group of network devices, thus permitting the group as a whole to receive an inbound message.

GROUP CHANNEL - a term used in the telephone industry to indicate the multiplexing together of 12 voice-grade channels into one.

GROUP CONTROL SYSTEM (GCS) - an IBM term referring to a system used with the VM operating system in the hosting of SNA-oriented subsystems.

GROUP SIGNAL - a term used in the telephone industry to indicate the span of a signal representing a group.

GROUP SWITCH - a type of switch incorporated into a multistage switching system that is in a stage other than the first. Thus, group switches are connected *only* to other switches.

GUARD TIME - a measurement of the unused time between the transmissions of a time-division multiplexer which is used for synchronization of the system.

GUARDBAND - refers to the frequencies located in between two adjacent communications bands, the purpose of which is to isolate the two channels from each other.

GUEST USER - a user given temporary access to a network or system.

GUIDED TRANSMISSION - transmissions in which the signals sent are confined to the immediate transport medium.

GUIDELINES FOR THE DEFINITION OF MANAGED OBJECTS (GDMO) - an ISO/OSI term defining the standards for describing managed objects and their associated traits and attributes.

H

HALF DUPLEX COMMUNICATIONS LINE - normally a two-wire line, or any communications line which operates in half-duplex mode.

HALF SESSION - an IBM term used in SNA to indicate the user functions at one end of a communications interaction.

HALF-DUPLEX (HDX) - refers to data transmission which may occur in either direction but in only one direction at a time.

HALF-DUPLEX CONTENTION MODE - a data communications mode in which all stations on a line are able to access the line when it is in an idle state. Since the stations involved are all in either a receive or send state at any one time, they utilize half-duplex communications.

HALF-DUPLEX FLIP-FLOP MODE - commonly known as modem turnaround, this term refers to a modem's ability to flip back and forth from sending mode to receiving mode.

HANDSHAKING - refers to the actual exchange of communications messages between two devices which enables them to manage all communications between them.

HARMONIC - a signal whose frequency is a whole-number multiple of another signal.

HARMONIC DISTORTION - refers to the distortion of a transmitted signal due to the creation and dissemination of harmonics during the transmission.

HASP - see *Houston Automatic Spooling System.*

HCF - see *Host Command Facility.*

HCTDS - see *High-Capacity Terrestrial Digital Service.*

HDLC - see *High-level Data Link Control.*

HDX - See *Half-Duplex.*

HEAD-END - a term used in broadband networking to indicate any device located at the end of a network which repeats a received signal in the return direction of the original signal and at a different frequency than was received.

HEADER - in data communications, the information (in the form of a packet, block, message or bits), which precedes the actual data being transmitted.

HEARTBEAT - a signaling function of Ethernet-type networks that indicates that the transceivers in the network are still active.

HERTZ (Hz) - the number of cycles per second of a given frequency.

HETROGENEOUS NETWORK - any network which contains components or protocols from different vendors.

HEXADECIMAL - a base-16 numbering system which proceeds 0, 1, 2, 3, 4, 5, 6, 7, 8, 9, A, B, C, D, E, F, 10, 11, 12, 13, etc.

HIERARCHICAL ARCHITECTURE - any network architecture which may be represented with an inverted tree diagram. Networks designed using this architecture employ network node connections in which a one-to-*n* parent/child relationship is used, thus allowing any node in the network to communicate only with its single parent or children.

HIERARCHICAL DISTRIBUTED PROCESSING - any distributed processing environment which is designed to operate through hierarchical architectural designs.

HIERARCHICAL ROUTING - any data communications routing technique in which the next node to be called on is a parent or child node.

HIGH-CAPACITY TERRESTRIAL DIGITAL SERVICE (HCTDS) - any digital transmission service designed to operate with a transfer rate greater than one million bits per second. TI, El, etc.

HIGH-LEVEL DATA LINK CONTROL (HDLC) - refers to an ISO-designed, bit-oriented protocol similar in design to IBM's SDLC. In HDLC, control-data bit patterns look very different from data bit patterns, thus reducing the number of potential errors.

HIGH-SPEED CIRCUIT - circuits designed to operate at speeds in excess of voice-rade circuits (i.e., greater than 20Kbps).

HIGH-SPEED LOCAL NETWORK (HSLN) - any local area network designed to operate at transfer rates greater than 20Mbps.

HOMOGENEOUS NETWORK - any network which utilizes the same protocols, procedures and management mechanisms throughout the network.

HOST - in data communications, any computer which provides communications services to other devices.

HOST COMMAND FACILITY (HCF) - an IBM term referring to the feature found on IBM's mainframe family of computers which allows a host user to access AS/400-based applications as if they were utilizing remote, 5250-type terminals.

HOT CARRIER - refers to a transmitter which is in permanent transmit mode due to some malfunction.

HOT POTATO ALGORITHM - refers to a data communications routing scheme in which messages are sent to the output line with the least amount of traffic already in line.

HOUSTON AUTOMATIC SPOOLING SYSTEM (HASP) - an IBM term referring to the half-duplex data-transfer protocol developed for batch processing arenas where multiple devices share a communications line. A Job Entry Subsystem (JES) for IBM's OS/MVS mainframes.

HSLN - see *High-Speed Local Network*.

HUB POLLING - a communications polling scheme in which the poll is sent in a circular manner to the first polling station and from there directly between terminal stations for the balance of time left in the polling sequence.

HYBRID NETWORK - any network design which includes smaller networks composed of different network topologies.

HYBRID SWITCHING - a type of message-switching utilizing a combination of packet- and circuit-switching techniques.

Hz - see *Hertz*.

I

IA5 - see *International Alphabet Number 5.*

IBM - see *International Business Machines.*

IBM INFORMATION NETWORK - IBM's public data network offering, which utilizes SNA.

IBM INTERCONNECT - an IBM term referring to a software package which allows non-IBM equipment to function in IBM environments.

ICA - see *International Communications Association* and *Integrated Communications Adapter.*

ICF - see *Intersystem Communications Function.*

ICF FILE - IBM term referring to a device file permitting two programs on different systems to communicate with each other.

ICMP - see *Internet Control Message Protocol.*

ICRCV - see *Interface Control Receive monitor.*

ICXMT - see *Interface Control Transmit monitor.*

ID - see *identification.*

IDA - see *Integrated Digital Access.*

IDAPI - see *International Database Access Programming Interface.*

IDCMA - see *Independent Data Communications Manufacturers Association.*

IDENTIFICATION (ID) - any method of recognizing an attempt by an entity to access a network. Some protocols use specific ID characters to achieve this end.

IDF - see *Intermediate Distribution Frame.*

IDI - see *Initial Domain Identifier.*

IDLE REPEAT REQUEST (IRQ) - refers to an error-control protocol also known as stop-and-wait, which allows for the half-duplex transmission of blocks of data. This methodology waits for a reply from the receiving station as to the success or failure of the last block transmitted.

IDLE STATE - refers to the condition of a network or other transmission system when no data signals are being sent or received.

IDLE TIMER - any device which measures the amount of idle state time.

IDN - see *Integrated Digital Network.*

IDU - see *Interface Data Unit.*

IEC - see *International Electrotechnical Commission.*

IEEE - see *Institute of Electrical and Electronics Engineer.*

IEN - see *Internet Engineering Notes.*

IFRB - see *International Frequency Registration Board.*

IFs - see *Interface Modules.*

IGMP - see *Internet Group Management Protocol.*

IGP - see *Interior Gateway Protocol.*

IMPEDANCE - in electrical engineering parlance, a measure of the opposition of current in an alternating current circuit. The combination of resistance, inductance and capacitance.

IMPEDANCE DISCONTINUITY - any point in a transmission medium at which the electrical characteristics of the medium change.

IMPLICIT RESERVATION - the reservation or allocation of a medium access interval to a particular device, without requiring the device to request the reservation. Used in medium access protocols.

IMPULSE NOISE - the pulsed form of electromagnetic noise.

IMS/DC - see *Information Management System/Data Communications.*

INBAND PROTOCOL - any protocol scheme which works within specifically assigned frequencies.

INBAND SIGNALING - any signaling scheme which works within specifically assigned frequencies.

INBOUND - in a dual-cable system, the cable which carries signals to the head-end.

INDEPENDENT DATA COMMUNICATIONS - refers to any data-communications control scheme in which the scheme operates independently of the character encoding being utilized.

INDEPENDENT DATA COMMUNICATIONS MANUFACTURERS ASSOCIATION (IDCMA) - U.S.-based organization which promotes the needs of non-AT&T aligned communications equipment manufacturers.

INDEPENDENT LOGICAL UNIT - a logical unit which can be activated without a command from the host.

INDIRECT STORE-AND-FORWARD DEADLOCK - networking problem which occurs when an intermediate node of a network is waiting for a network resource at one of the end nodes of the network, thus causing the nodes on either side of the intermediate node to be deadlocked.

INDUCTANCE - see *impedance*.

INDUSTRY STANDARD ARCHITECTURE (ISA) - refers to the specifications and recommendations agreed upon to allow open systems utilization of microcomputer architecture.

INFORMATION FIELD - any field in a protocol containing the user data to be transmitted. Also, the primary control of data information, variable-length field used in SDLC.

INFORMATION FRAME BIT-ORIENTED PROTOCOLS - as defined in data-link protocols, the segments of a transmission which hold user data.

INFORMATION FRAMES - refers to information fields and their associated ACKs/NACKs.

INFORMATION MANAGEMENT SYSTEM/DATA COMMUNICATIONS (IMS/DC) - an IBM term referring to a subsystem of IMS which provides data communications support.

INFORMATION SYSTEMS NETWORK (ISN) - AT&T-designed fiber-optic networking scheme.

INFORMATION TRANSFER CAPABILITY - the capability of exchanging information between any two points on a network.

INFORMATION TRANSFER COMMANDS AND RESPONSES - an IBM term referring to the command or response mode of SDLC for information frames which have been received or transmitted.

INFORMATION TRANSFER FORMAT - an IBM term used in SDLC to indicate the structure of data in an information frame and its sequence.

INFRARED TRANSMISSION - any communications scheme which utilizes infrared light as its transmission medium.

INITIAL DOMAIN IDENTIFIER (IDI) - refers to that portion of the OSI network address used to specify the domain.

INITIAL SEQUENCE NUMBER (ISN) - a sequence number defining the numbering of data octets. Set up during TCP/IP connection setup.

INSERTION LOSS - a measure of the loss of signal strength due to the attachment of devices with different impedances.

INSTITUTE OF ELECTRICAL AND ELECTRONICS ENGINEERS (IEEE) - professional organization which publishes data communications standards, among its many other activities.

INTEGRATED COMMUNICATIONS ADAPTER (ICA) - an IBM term describing a family of mainframe communications controllers.

INTEGRATED DIGITAL ACCESS (IDA) - any network facility providing access capabilities to a number of integrated data streams.

INTEGRATED DIGITAL NETWORK (IDN) - phrase used in circuit-switched networks to indicate the usage of digital methods of transmission and switching.

INTEGRATED INFORMATION SYSTEM - a networking scheme in which any device attached to the network may access any and all data stored within the network.

INTEGRATED SERVICE UNIT (ISU) - any device which combines the functions of both a channel service unit (CSU) and a data service unit (DSU) into one unit.

INTEGRATED SERVICES DIGITAL NETWORK (ISDN) - refers to a digital network in which data, voice, video, etc. are manipulated over a common physical circuit.

INTEGRATED SERVICES LOCAL NETWORK (ISLN) - any local area networking scheme which incorporates user services as a major component of its design.

INTEL - world-class manufacturer of semiconductors, located in Santa Clara, California.

INTELLIGENT HUB - networking hub containing decision-making capability.

INTERACTIVE DATA TRANSMISSION SYSTEM - refers to any data-transmission system which incorporates data-transfer capabilities in a real-time mode.

INTERACTIVE EXECUTIVE - IBM's version of UNIX.

INTERACTIVE MESSAGING - the a.k.a. name for voice-mail.

INTERACTIVE MODE - refers to the dialogue between DTEs consisting of inquiries and responses.

INTERACTIVE SYSTEM PRODUCTIVITY FACILITY/PROGRAM DEVELOPMENT FACILITY (ISPF/PDF) - an IBM term referring to this mainframe-based software package which allows 3270-compatible terminals to interact with TSO.

INTERACTIVE TERMINAL FACILITY (ITF) - IBM term referring to its asynchronous communications scheme which will permit AS/400 computers to interact with other applications.

INTERACTIVE TERMINAL INTERFACE (ITI) - device used to assemble and disassemble data packets in a CCITT X.25 network in which nonintelligent, asynchronous terminals are directly attached to the network.

INTERCHANGE CIRCUITS - any circuit designed to connect DCEs to DTEs.

INTERCHANGE CODE - any code sequence designed to facilitate the exchange of information between devices.

INTERCONNECTED NETWORK - any network which utilizes a bridge or gateway to connect to another network.

INTEREXCHANGE CARRIER (IXC) - another name for long-distance telephone companies.

INTERFACE - refers to a shared boundary or junction between two entities.

INTERFACE CONTROL RECEIVE MONITOR (ICRCV) - refers to any software module which has as its primary purpose the control of communications interfaces.

INTERFACE CONTROL TRANSMIT MONITOR (ICXMT) - refers to any software module which has as its primary purpose the control of an interface during data transmission.

INTERFACE DATA UNIT (IDU) - refers to the data structure passed between layers of the OSI reference model.

INTERFACE MODULES (IFs) - any software subroutine whose task is to manage the interface between two devices or software modules.

INTERFACE UNIT IDENTIFICATION - security scheme in which a transmitted message contains a description of the device which transmitted it.

INTERFERENCE - any unwanted signal which arrives at a destination along with the original signal.

INTERIOR GATEWAY PROTOCOL (IGP) - term used in TCP/IP referring to the protocol used to locate the most direct path through the Internet.

73

INTERLEAVING - refers to the process of taking sections of data from several sources and allocating them space on a single communications channel. See *multiplexing*.

INTERMEDIATE DISTRIBUTION FRAME (IDF) - any equipment designed to attach a communications device to a common-carrier local loop.

INTERMEDIATE SYSTEM - a router.

INTERMEDIATE SYSTEM-TO-INTERMEDIATE SYSTEM PROTOCOL (ISIS) - communications protocol designed to allow the routing of OSI and/or IP data.

INTERMEDIATE TEXT BLOCK (ITB) - a communications control character used to indicate the end of one block of text out of the number expected.

INTERNATIONAL ALPHABET NUMBER 5 (IA5) - CCITT-defined character set, similar to ASCII.

INTERNATIONAL BUSINESS MACHINES (IBM) - a.k.a. "Big Blue," the world's largest manufacturer of computer systems and associated devices and software.

INTERNATIONAL COMMUNICATIONS ASSOCIATION (ICA) - primarily a telecommunications research and education organization.

INTERNATIONAL DATABASE ACCESS PROGRAMMING INTERFACE (IDAPI) - a middleware standard created by IBM and Borland; designed to allow communications and data transfer between heterogeneous database management systems.

INTERNATIONAL ELECTROTECHNICAL COMMISSION (IEC) - international body defining standards for electrical/electronic devices.

INTERNATIONAL FREQUENCY REGISTRATION BOARD (IFRB) - agency whose domain includes the allocation of electromagnetic frequencies. Subset of ITU.

INTERNATIONAL STANDARDS ORGANIZATION (ISO) - international organization which outlines standards for scientific, technological and other activities. The Open Systems Interconnect reference model (OSI) is a product of the ISO.

INTERNATIONAL TELECOMMUNICATIONS UNION (ITU) - United Nations agency chartered with the development of unified international agreements on telecommunications. The Consultative Committee on International Telephony and Telegraphy (CCITT) is a subset of the ITU.

INTERNET - packet-switched and broadcast networks connected by gateways. Also the name for the world's largest network, which is TCP/IP based.

INTERNET CONTROL MESSAGE PROTOCOL (ICMP) - device which, using the DOD protocol, monitors and reports on a network's status.

INTERNET ENGINEERING NOTES (IEN) - Internet documentation of TCP/IP.

INTERNET GROUP MANAGEMENT PROTOCOL (IGMP) - Internet protocol used to convey group membership information.

INTERNET PROTOCOL (IP) - network-layer protocol allowing internetworking via a connectionless mode among packet-switching based networks. Primarily for routers and hosts.

INTERNETWORK FILE TRANSFER - the process of transferring a data file via a file-transfer protocol across two or more networks.

INTERNETWORK PACKET EXCHANGE (IPX) - subset of Xerox Corp.'s Xerox Network Services used by, among others, Novell in its NetWare product. It controls workstation-to-server and server-to-workstation technologies.

INTERNETWORK PROTOCOL STANDARD - a subset of the OSI reference model. Found on the network layer of the OSI model, its major tasks include internetworking, interoperability, intranetworking and link access.

INTERNETWORKING - the capacity of devices to communicate across more than one network.

INTEROPERABILITY - refers to the sharing, transmission and reception of data in an heterogeneous network.

INTERPACKET GAP - refers to the time between consecutive data packets.

INTERPROCESS COMMUNICATIONS (IPC) - any mechanism which will permit two programs to communicate with each other.

INTERREPEATER LINK (IRL) - a link between two network repeaters.

INTERRUPT CHARACTER - any communications control character which is used to cause a current process to be interrupted.

INTERRUPT REQUEST (IRQ) - a request for the running of a particular module of code.

INTERSYSTEM COMMUNICATIONS FUNCTION (ICF) - an IBM term referring to its operating system functions which permit program-to-program and system-to-system communications.

INTRASYSTEM COMMUNICATIONS - an IBM term which describes the capability of two programs in two different job streams to communicate with each other.

IP - see *Internet Protocol.*

IP ADDRESS - a 32-bit address identifying an IP network address.

IP DATAGRAM - the unit of data routed through IP networks.

IPC - see *Interprocess Communications.*

IPX - see *Internetwork Packet Exchange.*

IRL - see *Interrepeater Link.*

IRQ - see *Idle Repeat Request* and *Interrupt Request.*

ISA - see *Industry Standard Architecture.*

ISDN - see *Integrated Services Digital Network.*

ISIS - see *Intermediate System-to-Intermediate System protocol.*

ISLN - see *Integrated Services Local Network.*

ISN - see *Information Systems Network* and *Initial Sequence Number.*

ISO - see *International Standards Organization.*

ISOCHRONOUS COMMUNICATIONS - communications protocol which uses an integral number of unit intervals between asynchronous transmissions.

ISOCHRONOUS ETHERNET - a new, IBM-supported form of Ethernet, designed to handle applications such as multimedia and low-bandwidth teleconferencing. It works by adding 6Mbps ISDN channels, along which fixed-length packets are transmitted at constant speeds.

ISPF/PDF - see *Interactive System Productivity Facility/Program Development Facility.*

ISU - see *Integrated Service Unit.*

ITB - see *Intermediate Text Block.*

ITF - see *Interactive Terminal Facility.*

ITI - see *Interactive Terminal Interface.*

ITU - see *International Telecommunications Union.*

IX - see *Interactive Executive.*

IXC - see *Interexchange Carrier.*

J

J1 - a type of physical data link similar to T1.

JABBER - refers to an erroneous and purposeless transmission sent by a network device.

JACKET MATERIAL - the material used as the outer layer of insulation of a communications cable.

JAM SIGNAL - signal found in CSMA/CD networks which is used to ensure that all of the devices attached to the network will be informed if a collision is produced.

JCL - see *Job Control Language*.

JES - see *Job Entry System*.

JITTER - in analog communications, jitter refers to changes in phase or amplitude which occur in a rapid manner, thus causing noise on the circuit. In digital communications, it refers to minor changes in digital signals which alter the signal from the desired form.

JOB CONTROL LANGUAGE (JCL) - any of the family of high level languages used to interact with the operating system of a computer. On the AS/400 it's Control Language (CL).

JOB ENTRY SYSTEM (JES) - an IBM term referring to the successor of Remote Job Entry (RJE); it is a software product which enables the input, scheduling and output of submitted work on a host, from remote devices.

JOB TRANSFER AND MANIPULATION (JTM) - a protocol as defined in the OSI model which resides at the application layer and supplies the user processes with the ability to manipulate and transfer documents related to their jobs.

JTM - see *Job Transfer and Manipulation*.

JUMPER - a cable or wire used to establish a temporary connection or circuit where one did not previously exist.

K

Ka BAND - a band of frequencies ranging from 20-30GHz used in microwave and satellite transmissions.

KB - see *Kilobyte*.

Kbps - see *Kilobits per second*.

Kbyte - see *Kilobyte*.

KERBEROS - a security encryption service developed at the Massachusetts Institute of Technology to prevent intruders from discovering passwords to computer systems.

KERMIT - a file transfer protocol developed at Columbia University which uses sequence-numbered, variable-length data packets in conjunction with a block-check error-recovery scheme.

KEYBOARD/DISPLAY SESSION - host-based communications session where data targeted for the host is entered via keystrokes and data targeted for the user is presented in a buffer.

KEYBOARD/DISPLAY TERMINAL - a terminal (such as the IBM 3472) which can support one or more operator-to-host sessions.

KHz - see *KiloHertz*.

KILOBITS PER SECOND (Kbps) - one thousand bits per second.

KILOBYTE (KB, Kbyte) - Kilo- is a prefix meaning one-thousand. When used as a measurement of internal computer storage, a kilobyte is equal to 1,024 bytes; 1,000 bytes for external data storage.

KILOHERTZ (KHz) - one thousand cycles per second.

Ku Band - a band of frequencies ranging from 10-12GHz used in microwave transmissions.

L

L BAND - a range of frequencies in the 1GHz range used for satellite/microwave communications.

LAN ADMINISTRATOR - the person responsible for the administration of all LAN functions and equipment.

LAN MANAGER - any combination of hardware/software which together manages the performance of, or assists in the administration of, a LAN.

LAN PROTOCOL PERFORMANCE - refers to a measurement of the performance of selected LAN protocols operating under various traffic loads.

LAN/RM - see *Local Area Network Reference Model.*

LAP - see *Link Access Protocol.*

LAPB - see *Link Access Protocol-Balanced.*

LAPD - see *Link Access Protocol D-channel.*

LASER - see *Light Amplification by Stimulated Emission of Radiation.*

LAST-IN, FIRST-OUT (LIFO) - queuing scheme in which the most recent queue entry is the first one selected for processing. Contrast to *FIFO*.

LATA - see *Local Access Transport Area.*

LATE COLLISION - any number of failure conditions detected in a CSMA/CD network.

LATENCY - latency may be defined as either the delay created by the use of a physical device or of a software process; or the duration of time between a nodes asking for network access and receiving that access.

LAYER-INDEPENDENT DATA COMMUNICATIONS SYSTEM (LIDS) - system design in which layered architecture is used, but modified in such a way that each layer's contact with the layers adjacent to it is limited to the interface between the layers.

LAYERED ARCHITECTURE - any design which incorporates multiple functional layers, each stacked one on top of the other, in which each layer acts as a server to the layer above it. The OSI reference model is an example of layered architecture.

LBT - see *Listen Before Talk.*

LDM - see *Limited-Distance Modem.*

LEASED LINE - refers to a communications line which has been leased from a common carrier for the use of only one company or organization.

LEAST-COST ROUTING - routing scheme used in some packet-switched networks in order to route network traffic along the most economical route from source to destination.

LEC - see *Local Exchange Carrier.*

LEVEL 1 RELAY - a device designed to operate at the physical layer (layer 1) of the OSI reference model as a repeater.

LEVEL 2 RELAY - a device designed to operate at the data-link layer (layer 2) of the OSI reference model as a bridge.

LEVEL 3 RELAY - a device designed to operate at the network layer (layer 3) of the OSI reference model as a router.

LEVEL 7 RELAY - a device designed to operate at the application layer (layer 7) of the OSI reference model as a gateway.

LIDS - see *Layer-Independent Data Communications System.*

LIFO - see *Last-In, First-Out.*

LIGHT AMPLIFICATION BY STIMULATED EMISSION OF RADIATION (LASER) - a device for emitting light at a single, specific frequency, creating what is known as "coherent light".

LIGHT SPEED - a measure of the speed of light through a vacuum, approximately 186,324 miles per second.

LIGHTWAVE COMMUNICATIONS - any communications scheme in which light is used as the information carrier medium.

LIMITED PUBLIC NETWORK (LPN) - any digital data network whose range is roughly that of a metropolitan area.

LIMITED-DISTANCE MODEM (LDM) - also known as a short-haul modem, this type of modem receives, amplifies and corrects a DTE's signal and then retransmits it up to a few thousand feet away.

LINE - as defined for data communications, a line is a circuit connecting two or more points.

LINE CARD - any circuit card which can act as an interface between a line and a device.

LINE CONDITIONING - refers to any mechanism by which a communications or power line has its signal processed in order to meet specific characteristics of noise, error rates and so on. This is normally done only on leased lines, by the common carrier from whom the line was leased.

LINE CONFIGURATION - the arrangement of communications lines on multipoint or point-to-point network configurations.

LINE CONTROL - refers to the process for figuring out which device in a session is the receiver and which is the transmitter. Normally handled by the data-link control protocol.

LINE DISCIPLINE - also referred to as the data-link control, this is the line-control protocol used on a particular communications line to transmit or receive data.

LINE DRIVER - any hardware device designed to boost a transmitted signal over twisted-pair wiring, normally at distances of up to 2,000 feet and speeds of up to 19,200bps.

LINE GROUP - any logical grouping of communications lines which may be activated or inactivated as a group.

LINE HIT - any electromagnetic noise which disrupts normal communications line activities.

LINE LEVEL - a measurement of signal strength at a given point on a communications line, as measured in decibels.

LINE LOADING - refers to a measurement of the maximum capacity of a communications circuit as actually used during a given period of time.

LINE MONITOR - any data communications testing device which may be attached to a communications line in order to display or store the data transmitted over that line to validate and observe the transmission.

LINE SPEED - a measurement of the speed at which a line may transmit data while maintaining certain quality standards.

LINE TRACE - normally, a network control program software function which allows users to collect diagnostic information about a communications line.

LINE TRAINING TIME - a measure of the time required to change transmission directions on a half-duplex communications line.

LINE TURNAROUND (LTA) - as defined in half-duplex communications, the process of changing a modem from a receiving to a transmitting state.

LINE-CONTROL COMPUTER - any computer whose dedicated purpose is managing the interface functions for communications lines.

LINE-OF-SIGHT - as used in data communications, this refers to transmission schemes in which the transmitter and receiver must have an unobstructed path between them. Microwave transmissions, for example, must be line-of-sight.

LINE-SHARING DEVICE - any hardware device designed to allow multiple devices to share a single communications line (i.e., a multiplexer).

LINEAR PREDICTIVE CODING (LPC) - any method of coding used in the digitization of analog signals which is able to predict the direction the analog signal will take and thus reduce the number of samples required to digitally capture the waveform.

LINK - a portion or section of a line between two specific points.

LINK ACCESS PROTOCOL (LAP) - the policies used to start, stop, and control link level transmissions, as in SDLC, for example.

LINK ACCESS PROTOCOL D CHANNEL (LAPD) - a link-control protocol scheme related to ISDN and based on HDLC in which the D-channel of HDLC is used for channel control and addressing.

LINK ACCESS PROTOCOL-BALANCED (LAPB) - a CCITT bit-oriented, data-link protocol used in packet-switched networks. Any station may begin transmitting without obtaining permission from a network control point.

LINK MANAGEMENT - all elements required for the proper functioning and control of transmission links in a network.

LINK RELIABILITY - see *Mean Time Between Failures*.

LINK STATION ADDRESS - a station's send address (which must be unique) and receiving address which may not be unique if more than one is used.

LINK-ATTACHED - describing any type of device connection which uses a communications line rather than a direct channel attachment method.

LISTEN BEFORE TALK (LBT) - that section of CSMA/CD which stipulates that a node which wants to transmit must first listen to determine whether or not the transmission medium is free. If so, it transmits. If not, it waits.

LISTEN WHILE TALK (LWT) - that section of CSMA/CD which stipulates that a node which wants to transmit must listen for a collision during its transmission, even if the medium is free.

LLC - see *Logical Link Control*.

LMI - see *Local Management Interface*.

LOAD BALANCING - any process in which multiple service units are equally assigned.

LOADED LINE - any communications telephone line in which coils are utilized to reduce distortion and to increase the speed of the line.

LOBE - as used in IBM Token-Ring networks, a piece of cable which connects a device to an access unit.

LOBE RECEPTACLE - as used in IBM Token-Ring networks, a wiring concentrator outlet which connects a lobe.

LOCAL ACCESS TRANSPORT AREA (LATA) - refers to that geographic area assigned to a local exchange telephone carrier (LEC). Broadly speaking, one area code is equal to a LATA's area of responsibility.

LOCAL AREA DATA SET - see *limited-distance modem*.

LOCAL AREA NETWORK (LAN) - any network whose geographical area is limited to a particular building, campus or other such structure, and is capable of data transmission at rates from 2Mbps to 100+Mbps.

LOCAL AREA NETWORK REFERENCE MODEL (LAN/RM) - generic phrase used to refer to the IEEE 802 specifications.

LOCAL BUSY - the state of an adapter which occurs when it can't deal with additional frame activity for one or more of its link stations.

LOCAL EXCHANGE CARRIER (LEC) - a common carrier whose charter is the supplying of intraLATA services; e.g., the Bell operating companies.

LOCAL LOOP - that circuit which connects your telephone with the central telephone office.

LOCAL LOOPBACK - a test designed to validate the local connection between devices such as modems and their associated DTES.

LOCAL MANAGEMENT INTERFACE (LMI) - refers to a group of specifications, developed by a consortium of companies, for the communication of management information between a network and its associated user devices.

LOCAL NAME - as contrasted to *global name*, a name known to only one node in a network and not known by the rest of the nodes of the network.

LOCAL SESSION - the number assigned to each NetBios session established by an adapter.

LOCAL TOKEN BRIDGE (LTB) - any bridge between token-ring networks which doesn't utilize wide area communications facilities.

LOCALTALK - Apple Computer's communications protocol for its Macintosh line of computers.

LOCKOUT - a network condition in which a network device will inhibit its own usage or that of the resources it manages in order to ensure their integrity.

LOG FILES - a group of files in which data has been written ("logged") for future reference. These files may contain error information, transaction data and so on.

LOGICAL BYTE - a byte which is a specific number of bits in length.

LOGICAL CHANNEL IDENTIFICATION - refers to the name assigned to a virtual circuit or call for the duration of the call or session.

LOGICAL CONNECTION - an IBM term used in SNA to indicate the connection between two Network Addressable Units (NAUs), thus rendering a virtual circuit connection.

LOGICAL LINK CONTROL (LLC) - that section of a procedure or protocol tasked with controlling link-level data transmissions.

LOGICAL TOPOLOGY - refers to the arrangement of network components in a logical manner in order to indicate the movement of signals from one point to another, regardless of the physical arrangement of those components.**LAN** - see *Local Area Network*.

LOGICAL UNIT (LU) - as defined by IBM, the logical end user of a communications service. There are seven types (numbered 0-7) of LUs:

Type 1: Printers, readers, console diskette support; user-definable; a catch-all.

Type 2: 3270-type terminals.

Type 3: 3270-type printers.

Type 4: Peer-to-peer communications devices using SNA character streams.

Type 5: Reserved for IBM.

Type 6: Program-to-program support. APPC is LU 6.2.

Type 7: Sessions from application to interactive CRT terminals.

LONGHAUL - any transmission service with a range that exceeds 50 miles.

LONGHAUL MODEMS - modems designed to operate at distances in excess of 10 miles.

LONGITUDINAL REDUNDANCY CHECK (LRC) - error detection/correction scheme in which a check bit value in a check character is calculated by adding up the data bits in the same character position.

LOOP CONFIGURATION - another name for a ring network.

LOOP START - referring to the start-up procedures used to initiate a ring network.

LOOP TRANSMISSION - an IBM term used in SNA to indicate the ability to start hub polling. The loop controller (the primary station) is able to send command frames to any node in the loop.

LOOPBACK - any method for sending signals on a round trip--from a source to a destination and back again--in order to measure the signal or validate the data transmitted.

LOOPBACK ADAPTER - test device used in loopback tests, it interfaces between the DTE's and DCE's connection.

LOOPBACK TEST - see *Loopback*.

LOOSELY COUPLED - an IBM term used to refer to computers directly attached via their I/O channels.

LOW FREQUENCY - the band of frequencies below 3MHz.

LOW PASS - refers to the highest frequency which may be passed through a specific filter.

LOW-ENTRY NETWORKING - an IBM term referring to a form of SNA used with midrange computers.

LOW-LEVEL PROTOCOLS - all layers of the OSI reference model which are below the network layer.

LOWER SIDEBAND - those frequencies below the carrier frequency.

LPC - see *Linear Predictive Coding*.

LPN - see *Limited Public Network*.

LRC - see *Longitudinal Redundancy Check*.

LTA - see *Line Turnaround*.

LTB - see *Local Token Bridge*.

LU - see *Logical Unit*.

LU 6.2 - an IBM term used to refer to the peer-to-peer protocol used in SNA which permits devices to communicate with each other directly without one of the devices assuming the role of a primary station.

LU-TO-LU SESSION - an IBM SNA session in which users of the network can communicate with each other in a dynamic manner and in such a way as to render the network invisible to them except for knowing the address of the node they wish to communicate with.

LWT - see *Listen While Talk*.

M

M BIT - an X.25 bit which indicates that a message has More data to come.

M24 - a multiplexer used in Tl circuits to connect 64Kbps lines to a central switch.

M44 - a multiplexer used in Tl circuits to connect a T1 line of a particular protocol to another Tl line of a different protocol.

MAC - see *Medium Access Control*.

MAIL EXCHANGER - any system designed to route mail into a locally administered Internet.

MAIL SERVER - a computer dedicated to electronic mail services.

MAILGRAM - any electronic mail message which is transmitted with no validation of actual delivery.

MAIN - a PBX or similar device into which multiple PBXs are routed.

MAIN NETWORK ADDRESS (MNA) - an IBM term used to designate the logical unit address used in sessions between LUs and Session Service Control Points (SSCPs).

MAKE/BREAK SIGNAL - refers to the state of an asynchronous communications line which is maintained in a zero state for longer than the time of other character codes and thus ends in a framing error.

MAN - see *Metropolitan Area Network*.

MANCHESTER CODE - digital data-coding scheme which utilizes a transition in the middle of each bit time and results in a zero being coded in the last portion of bit time and a one being coded in the first portion of the bit time.

MANUAL ANSWER - as opposed to auto-answer, a line type which needs human intervention in order to receive an incoming call.

MANUAL CALL - as opposed to auto-call, a line type which needs human intervention to place a call.

MAPPED CONVERSATION - an IBM term referring to a temporary connection between an APPC session and an application program in which the system supplies data-formatting information.

MAPPING - refers to the logical relationship of a set of network values with those in a different network.

MARK - any communications signal which results in a circuit kept in the "1" bit mode while the communications line is itself in an idle state.

MARK PARITY - refers to the state in which the parity bit is sustained in the "1" bit state.

MARK/SPACE SIGNAL - the change in a communications circuit from a "1" bit, or mark state, to a "0" bit or space state.

MASTER CLOCK - the primary source of all device timing in a network.

MASTER CONTROL NUMBERING - any message, frame, etc., numbering method controlled by a master source.

MASTER CONTROL PROGRAM (MCP) - the operating system for Unisys computers.

MASTER STATION - any network station which possesses immediate control over other network stations.

MATRIX SWITCH - any circuit-switching mechanism in which every incoming line has the potential of being connected to every outgoing line by means of a matrix of connections.

MAU - see *Medium Attachment Unit* and *Multistation Access Unit* and *Medium Adapter Unit*.

MAXIMUM HOPS - parameter used in packet-switched networks to limit the number of intermediate nodes a packet may travel through on the way to its destination.

MAXIMUM SEGMENT SIZE - a term used in TCP/IP networks to refer to the maximum allowed size of the data portion of any segment transmitted.

MAXIMUM TRANSMISSION UNIT (MTU) - denoting the biggest datagram which may be transmitted across a particular network technology.

MB - see *Megabyte*.

Mbps - see *Megabits per second*.

Mbyte - see *Megabyte*.

MCA - see *Micro-Channel Architecture*.

MCP - see *Master Control Program*.

MEAN TIME BETWEEN FAILURES (MTBF) - mathematical average time in hours between failures of an entity.

MEDIUM - refers to any physical apparatus used to transmit signals.

MEDIUM ACCESS CONTROL (MAC) - any methodology which provides for orderly transmission of data between devices over a common medium. Defined as the physical layer in the OSI reference model.

MEDIUM ADAPTER UNIT (MAU) - 1) an IBM term referring to its Token-Ring device which allows users to build small token-rings without the need for interconnecting wiring; 2) any device whose job is to attach another device to a transmission medium.

MEDIUM ATTACHMENT UNIT (MAU) - any device designed to attach a device to a transmission medium.

MEGABIT (Mb) - one million bits.

MEGABITS PER SECOND (Mbps) - one million bits per second.

MEGABYTE (MB, Mbyte) - 1,048,576 eight-bit bytes.

MEGAHERTZ (MHz) - one million cycles per second.

MESH TOPOLOGY - any networking scheme in which every node in the network is directly attached to every other node in the network.

MESSAGE - refers to any group of characters which is transmitted as a whole unit.

MESSAGE FORMATTING - the process of locating data elements within a message in a precise manner.

MESSAGE NUMBER - see *Message Sequence Number.*

MESSAGE ROUTING - refers to the process of choosing which circuits a message will be transmitted to.

MESSAGE SEQUENCE NUMBER - a number which is used to uniquely identify the sequence in which a message has been transmitted or received.

MESSAGE STORE - storage system in X.400 electronic mail networks that accepts delivery of messages addressed to a specific user.

MESSAGE SWITCH - any point in a communications scheme at which a message is switched onto its destination's circuit.

MESSAGE SWITCHING - the handling and routing of a message to its final destination in which no physical path for the routing is selected in advance.

MESSAGE SYNCHRONIZATION - any scheme employed to indicate the start or end of a message.

MESSAGE TRANSFER AGENT (MTA) - as used in X.400 electronic mail networks, it forwards messages between network agents.

MESSAGE TRANSFER SYSTEM (MTS) - as used in X.400 electronic mail networks, it's the routes available to Message Transfer Agents.

MESSAGE UNIT - an IBM term referring to the section of data passed to and processed by a specific layer of IBM's SNA network design.

MESSAGE-FRAMED DATA - any data to be transmitted which has had control characters attached to it so that it may be transmitted as a complete message frame.

MESSAGE-HANDLING SYSTEM (MHS) - also referred to as X.400, this is a protocol of the applications layer of the OSI reference model chartered with the responsibility of exchanging electronic mail.

MESSAGE-SWITCHED NETWORK - any network design incorporating message-switching.

METROPOLITAN AREA NETWORK (MAN) - normally defined as a network whose boundaries are contained with a 50-mile radius.

MHS - see *Message-Handling System*.

MHz - see *MegaHertz*.

MICRCOM NETWORKING PROTOCOL (MNP) - popular protocol used by a wide variety of modem manufacturers.

MICRO-CHANNEL ARCHITECTURE (MCA) - an IBM term referring to its design of the Micro-channel bus product.

MICRO-CHANNEL BUS - an IBM term referring to its 32-bit expansion bus designed for use on the PS/2 family of personal computers.

MICROSECOND - one-millionth of a second.

MICROWAVE - a range of frequencies between 1GHz to 30GHz, used for line-of-sight telecommunications.

MICROWAVE HOP - the interval between one microwave relay tower and the next.

MICROWAVE RADIO - machines which generate microwave carrier signals for data transmission.

MICROWAVE REPEATERS - devices which receive microwave transmissions and then retransmit them. Normally located at a maximum of 40 kilometers apart or closer if objects in the path of the microwave network will interfere with proper transmission.

MIDSPLIT - frequency-division scheme used in some broadband networks.

MIF - see *Minimum Internetworking Functionality*.

MILLAR CODING - data-encoding scheme used over twisted-pair wiring.

MILLISECOND - one-thousandth of a second.

MINIMUM INTERNETWORKING FUNCTIONALITY (MIF) - refers to the fundamental functions of a LAN node capable of attachment to a WAN, as defined by the ISO.

MINIMUM SPANNING TREE (MST) - any spanning tree network design which yields the lowest overall cost.

MNA - see *Main Network Address*.

MNP - see *Microcom Networking Protocol*.

MODE - one of the major conditions of functioning in data communications. The three modes are: Information, Operating and Synchronization.

MODE DESCRIPTION - an IBM term referring to an APPC device object outlining session limits and characteristics.

MODEM - a device designed to process a digital signal so that the signal may be transmitted over analog communications lines. Contraction of "MODulate" and "DEModulate".

MODEM CARRIER - a continuous signal transmitted by a modem having the capacity of being modulated. Also called a *carrier*.

MODEM ELIMINATOR - a device designed to take the place of a modem for data transmission over short distances.

MODEM EMULATOR - any device which emulates the functions of a modem.

MODEM POOLING - a situation in which a single called number is able to access a number of modems in a hunt-group concept similar to that of telephone systems.

MODEM SELF-TEST - refers to a group of tests that a modem is capable of performing on itself, many of which are performed when the modem is powered on.

MODEM SET COMMANDS - any series of control commands which aid a modem in setting its processing parameters (i.e., bps, parity, and so forth).

MODEM SIMULATOR - see *modem emulator*.

MODEM SYNCHRONIZATION TIME - a measure of the duration required for a modem to align itself so that it's capable of receiving data from a sending modem.

MODEM TRAINING TIME - see *modem synchronization time*.

MODEM TURNAROUND (MTA) - a measure of the duration required for a modem to change its state (receiving/transmitting or vice versa) in half-duplex transmissions.

MODEM-SHARING UNIT - any device designed so as to allow a modem to be shared by

MODULAR TELEPHONE JACK - any of the family of connectors designed to plug in single-line or multiple-line telephones.

MODULATED SIGNAL - any electrical signal which has had one of its characteristics altered in order to convey information.

MODULATION - refers to the process of changing the properties of a signal. AM refers to Amplitude Modulation, FM to Frequency Modulation.

MODULATION RATE - may be expressed as the reciprocal of the briefest interval between consecutive events of a modulated signal.

MODULATOR - any device designed to modulate a carrier signal.

MONITOR - an IBM term used in Token-Ring networks to indicate the function needed to start token transmissions, provide error recovery, etc.

MONITOR BIT - a bit used in some messaging schemes which is utilized in the detection or correction of a device failure.

MPS - see *Multiple Port Sharing*.

MSNF - see *Multisystem Networking Facility*.

MST - see *Minimum Spanning Tree*.

MTA - see *Modem Turnaround* and *Message Transfer Agent*.

MTBF - see *Mean Time Between Failures*.

MTS - see *Message Transfer System*.

MTU - see *Maximum Transmission Unit*.

MULTI-HOMED HOST - a term used in TCP/IP networking to designate a host attached to more than one network and requiring multiple IP addresses.

MULTIACCESS CONNECTION - connection scheme in which any network station may transmit data to any number of network stations. Ethernet (IEEE 802.3) bus topology.

MULTIBIT MODULATION - any of the modulation methodologies in which several bits are encoded upon a single signal instance.

MULTICAST - refers to the process of sending a message on a network so that every node of the network receives the message.

MULTIDROP LIMITATION - refers to a measure of the number of stations which may be attached to a line before the operational characteristics of the line are eroded to an unacceptable level.

MULTIDROP LINE - communications circuit scheme in which multiple stations are connected to the same physical line.

MULTILEAVING - refers to a communications methodology in which a single line and buffer are used to accommodate multiple devices at each end of the line. Since multiple messages are interspersed during transmission, the receiving end allocates the messages to the intended recipient.

MULTILEVEL BINARY - signal-encoding scheme in which multiple bits are encoded onto a single signal element by means of employing different levels of the signal.

MULTIMODE FIBER - a type of fiber-optic cable designed to carry multiple frequencies at the same time.

MULTIMODE GRADED INDEX - refers to a form of fiber-optic cable which has the characteristic of having its index of refraction varied radially, not in a fixed manner. This feature allows the fiber-optic cable to compensate for the differential speed of light reflected through it.

MULTIPLE HOPS - any networking situation in which a message must travel through multiple nodes before its final destination. The distance between each of the intervening nodes is referred to as a *hop*.

MULTIPLE PORT SHARING (MPS) - an IBM term describing an arrangement for short-hold mode operations in which the first call and any subsequent recalls for a group of DTE's are routed to whichever port is available within a group of ports.

MULTIPLE ROUTING - any routing scheme in which a message is transmitted to more than one destination by way of the same route, or along different routes.

multiple transmitting devices.

MULTIPLE VIRTUAL STORAGE (MVS) - an IBM term referring to its mainframe-based operating system designed for online, multiuser operations.

MULTIPLE-ADDRESS MESSAGE - network message addressed to more than one destination.

MULTIPLE-DOMAIN SNA NETWORK - an IBM term referring to an SNA network with more than one domain.

MULTIPLEXER (MUX) - any device capable of combining signals from many sources into a common signal and then sorting the interleaved messages out again at their destination.

MULTIPOINT CONFIGURATION - any communications scheme which utilizes a multidrop line scenario.

MULTIPOINT LINE - see *Multidrop Line*.

MULTIPOINT REPEATER - any repeater which gathers transmissions from one channel and retransmits them on one or more new channels.

MULTIPORT TRANSCEIVER - a network device permitting multiple devices to be attached to one LAN transceiver.

MULTISTATION ACCESS UNIT (MAU) - any network device which is designed to allow for the attachment of multiple stations onto a LAN.

MULTISTATION CIRCUIT - any circuit design which allows for multiple stations to share a common circuit.

MULTISYSTEM NETWORKING FACILITY (MSNF) - an IBM term referring to software-based communications tool for allowing multiple 370-type hosts to control network functions and configurations.

MULTITAP - a directional coupler, a splitter and two or more output connections combined into one component.

MULTITHREADING - the capacity of a system to handle more than one transaction concurrently.

MULTIUSER SYSTEM - normally, a time-sharing system which permits multiple users to access a system at the same time.

MUX - see *multiplexer*.

MVS - see *Multiple Virtual Storage*.

MVS/ENTERPRISE SYSTEM ARCHITECTURE (MVS/ESA) - an IBM term referring to its 309x-based version of SNA.

MVS/ESA - see *MVS/Enterprise System Architecture*.

MVS/SP - an IBM term referring to a low-end version of MVS.

MVS/XA - an IBM term referring to its mid-line version of MVS.

MVT - an IBM term referring to a S/360-based operating system.

N

N-TYPE CONNECTOR - refers to the group of threaded end connection devices created for use with coaxial cable.

NAA - see *Network Application Architecture*.

NAC - see *Network Access Controller* and *Not Acknowledge Character*.

NAK - see *Negative Acknowledgment*.

NAME KNOWLEDGE - refers to the nodes of a network which possess a list of the names of other objects in the network and are capable of performing message-routing functions based upon those names.

NAME SERVER - refers to the specific network node which manages naming services for the other network nodes.

NAME STRUCTURE - the unique syntax relied upon to construct route path naming.

NAMED MAILSLOTS - an IBM term used in OS/2 to indicate a method for remote processors to transmit data to one another by name.

NAMED PIPES - any channel capable of full-duplex traffic between different processes or different computers via the establishment of virtual sessions.

NANOSECOND - one-billionth of a second.

NARROWBAND - the bandwidths less than 1200 Hz. AKA subvoice grade range.

NARROWBAND ISDN - the CCITT's original name for ISDN.

NAS - see *Network Application Support*.

NATIONAL INSTITUTE OF STANDARDS AND TECHNOLOGY (NIST) - the agency of the U.S. government responsible for telecommunication and networking standards.

NATIONWIDE PUBLIC NETWORKS - form of data network in which a network user at one node may establish a session with any other network node(s).

NAU - see *network-addressable unit*.

NAUN - see *Nearest Active Upstream Neighbor*.

NCC - see *Network Control Center.*

NCCF - see *Network Communications Control Facility.*

NCL - see *Network Command Language.*

NCP - see *NetWare Core Protocol,* and *Network Control Program.*

NDIS - see *Network Driver Interface Specification.*

NDT - see *Net Data Throughput.*

NEAR END CROSSTALK (NEXT) - refers to the noise created by the transfer of energy between circuits located at the beginning (sometimes called the source end or near end) of a transmission link.

NEAR INSTANTANEOUS COMPANDING (NIC) - the extremely rapid quantizing of an analog into a digital signal.

NEAREST ACTIVE UPSTREAM NEIGHBOR (NAUN) - an IBM term used in Token-Ring networking to indicate the active ring station sending tokens and frames to the network.

NEEDLE PACKET - a network packet used in virtual circuit networks which moves along a preplanned route, informs each intermediate node of its participation in the route and establishes a virtual circuit.

NEGATIVE ACKNOWLEDGMENT (NAK) - a transmission control character used in protocols such as bisync to inform the transmitter that the receiver has detected an error in the last transmission.

NEGATIVE BIAS - a form of distortion found in signaling systems in which the negative bit signals are increased in length versus the positive bit signals.

NEGOTIATION - any scheme which allows two network nodes to determine the parameters to be used on a virtual circuit for data transmission.

NET DATA THROUGHPUT (NDT) - the actual rate at which data is transmitted on a channel. Expressed normally in bits per second, this is not the theoretical rate for the channel, but the actual data transfer rate.

NETBIOS - see *Network Basic Input/Output System.*

NETVIEW - an IBM term referring to its network management software scheme created to support network management operations on IBM network (or compatible) platforms. A version is available for PCs (Netview/PC) which allows non-SNA network architectures.

NETWARE - Novell's LAN operating system.

NETWARE CORE PROTOCOL (NCP) - a Novell term referring to the policies used by a file server to process requests from network nodes.

NETWARE-LOADABLE MODULE (NLM) - Novell term referring to a program module which is loadable and executable by NetWare.

NETWORK - generic term pertaining to any group of interconnected devices which utilizes an architecture that negates the need for every device to be physically connected to every other device.

NETWORK ACCESS CONTROLLER (NAC) - any device which functions as a network access point.

NETWORK ACCESS LAYER - any layer of a network model which is charged with the following tasks: error detection and recovery, service-level determination, message blocking, message relaying, patch establishment, node-to-node communications establishment and at least rudimentary management functions for the above.

NETWORK ADDRESS - any unique ID of a network object, used primarily to establish a route between logical units. The address may be a name, number, code-sequence or combination of these. In TCP/IP networking, the 32-bit IP address of a system.

NETWORK ADMINISTRATOR - the person charged with the tasks of overseeing and maintaining a network.

NETWORK APPLICATION ARCHITECTURE (NAA) - any network architecture which is designed to permit the maximum interoperability at the application layer of its design. IBM's System Application Architecture (SAA) is an example of this concept.

NETWORK APPLICATION SUPPORT (NAS) - software routines used in network-related systems to perform network-related tasks.

NETWORK ARCHITECTURE - a plan for a network which includes the hardware, software, interfaces and guidelines necessary to implement the network design.

NETWORK BASIC INPUT/OUTPUT SYSTEM (NETBIOS) - DOS-compatible software routines used to manage various network functions.

NETWORK COMMAND LANGUAGE (NCL) - refers to any computer language which includes functions to handle networking-related issues.

NETWORK COMMUNICATIONS CONTROL FACILITY (NCCF) - an IBM term used in SNA networking to denote a facility which allows operator control over multiple domain networks.

NETWORK CONTROL CENTER (NCC) - the physical installation which is the main control point for a network and home to the network management personnel.

NETWORK CONTROL PROGRAM (NCP) - as defined for IBM networks, the NCP is a software system which permits the control of the physical network functions, the transmission functions and the bit manipulation, pooling, routing, error-control and code-translation functions.

NETWORK DIAMETER - a measurement of the shortest path between the two most physically distant nodes in a network.

NETWORK DICTIONARY - refers to a network-based list of all objects known to the network, as well as the definitions of the objects.

NETWORK DRIVER INTERFACE SPECIFICATION (NDIS) - standard interface specification developed by Microsoft and 3Com for use in DOS and OS/2 environments to access data-link layer services within those environments.

NETWORK FILE SYSTEM (NFS) - a protocol for file transfer commonly used on TCP/IP networks.

NETWORK INFORMATION SOURCE (NIS) - any network node which is addressable by any other network node and has information which may be useful to them.

NETWORK INTERFACE - any interface scheme or device designed to be placed between a network and a computer.

NETWORK INTERFACE CARD (NIC) - a printed-circuit card used to attach a network device to the network's transmission medium.

NETWORK INTERFACE UNIT (NIU) - see *Network Interface Card*.

NETWORK LAYER - that portion of a network architecture charged with end-to-end network data routing.

NETWORK LOGICAL DATA MANAGER (NLDM) - an IBM term referring to the software product for network performance monitoring and network problem determination.

NETWORK MANAGEMENT PROGRAM - any program designed to allow a network manager to meet the networking needs of his network user community.

NETWORK MANAGEMENT SOFTWARE - any software designed to control network functions within the network.

NETWORK MANAGEMENT SYSTEM (NMS) - any group of integrated software programs providing network management functions.

NETWORK MANAGEMENT VECTOR TRANSPORT (NMVT) - an IBM term used to refer to the management protocol used by the network management system.

NETWORK MODELING - network simulation models or algorithm routines used by a network designed to build a network model.

NETWORK OBJECT - an entity (such as a program, processor or network device) which is capable of being manipulated by defined operations.

NETWORK OPERATION (OPERATING) SYSTEM (NOS) - any software system designed to consolidate network functions.

NETWORK PROBLEM DETERMINATION AID (NPDA) - as defined for an IBM environment, an IBM-designed software system which is capable of collecting, storing, analyzing and reporting network problem information.

NETWORK PROTOCOL - the data exchange criteria, format designs, software interface designs and timing criteria and any other required parameters which dictate the exchange of data on a given network.

NETWORK PROTOCOL DATA UNIT (NPDU) - a term associated with the OSI reference model; it refers to the form in which the network layer formats data.

NETWORK REDUNDANCY - a network condition in which there are more connection links than necessary to provide for node interconnection. The theory behind network redundancy is that if one of the connection links fails, another is available to replace it with minimal impact to the network.

NETWORK SECURITY - a generic term referring to procedures such as passwords, data encryption and authentication protocols which are designed to restrict access to a network to authorized users.

NETWORK SERVER - generic term describing any network node which performs a specific task for other network nodes.

NETWORK SERVICE ACCESS POINT (NSAP) - a network-layer interface point found in layered network architectures which is a logical and addressable point at which network services may be obtained.

NETWORK SERVICES - a very general term referring to all services of which a network is capable which are not directly related to the information-processing services performed by the network nodes themselves.

NETWORK SOLICITOR - an IBM term used in VTAM networking which indicates the process of monitoring network terminals for activity.

NETWORK STATISTICS - a broad term referring to all of the performance and operational statistics and measurements of activity which the network management software collects for evaluation.

NETWORK TERMINATION - the process, required in many transmission media, of placing a termination device (such as a BNC cap) at the end of network media to end the transmission of, or limit the interference caused by, network transmissions.

NETWORK TOPOLOGY - refers to the structure and layout of the nodes, links, termination and (in many cases) geometric description of a network. Star, ring, undefined, and bus are common terms referring to a network's topology.

NETWORK TRANSPARENCY - allowing for the fact that contemporary networks may be called upon to transmit all manner of information (i.e., video, text, graphics), network transparency is any method which allows for the seamless transport of information on a network. In many cases, special bit sequences are used to accomplish this.

NETWORK VIRTUAL TERMINAL - similar in concept to a logical file on an AS/400, a network virtual terminal is a "pseudo device" created to facilitate the transfer of information in a network. The virtual controllers and devices created with Display Station Pass-through are network virtual devices.

NETWORK-ADDRESSABLE UNIT (NAU) - an IBM term referring to a logical or physical unit or a system service control point in an SNA network responsible for network data movement and management.

NEURAL NETWORKING - refers to those types of networks designed to simulate the functions of the human brain, normally through parallel network design.

NEXT - see *Near-End Crosstalk*.

NFS - see *Network File System*.

NIC - see *Near Instantaneous Companding* and *Network Interface Card*.

NIS - see *Network Information Source*.

NIST - see *National Institute of Standards and Technology*.

NIU - see *Network Interface Unit*.

NLDM - see *Network Logical Data Manager*.

NLM - see *NetWare-Loadable Module*.

NMS - see *Network Management System*.

NMVT - see *Network Management Vector Transport*.

NO PARITY - refers to any communications transmission scheme in which parity bits are not used for error detection and control.

NODAL PROCESSOR - synonymous with multiplexer in Tl transmission technology.

NODE - any point in a network at which a device performs a network function (i.e., printing, switching, routing, or network device linkage).

NODE ADDRESS - any unique form of identifying a specific node within a network.

NODE DELAY - the amount of time a packet must wait at a network node before it can be sent to its next destination.

NODE NAME - any user-defined name for a node within a network; normally translated into a node address for use by the network.

NOISE - the additional electrical interference not originally encoded on an electrical waveform. Noise can be created by crosstalk, thermal conditions, electrical impulses or other reasons. Noise is normally measured in decibels.

NONADAPTIVE ROUTING - any routing scheme which is incapable of adapting to changes in the network.

NONBLOCKING NETWORKS - any network in which transmitted frames of data are not grouped into blocks.

NONCONTENTION NETWORKING METHODS - network schemes such as token-ring which work on a circuit-sharing basis and employ a noncontention (read: access-based) access scheme. Polling of AS/400 direct-attached terminals is also an example of this.

NONCONTINUOUS CARRIER - carrier-manipulation strategy in which the carrier wave is dropped when no data is being transmitted over the link.

NONINTERACTIVE DATA TRANSMISSION - batch-mode transmission requiring no human intervention.

NONRETURN TO ZERO (NRZ) - nonreturn to zero is a transmission scheme in which electrical zero is not used to define a binary one or zero. Instead, two unique electrical states define them.

NONRETURN TO ZERO INVERTED (NRZI) - nonreturn to zero inverted does not use electrical zero to define a binary one or zero; instead, binary zeros alter the electrical state of the transmission and binary ones do not.

NONROUTING NODE - normally an end node in a network, this term refers to any network node incapable of routing functions.

NONSEQUENCED FORMAT - a format for transmitting message packets over a network in which no sequence numbering is used to facilitate error correction.

NONSWITCHED LINE - a point-to-point line.

NONSWITCHED NETWORK - any network design in which dial-up or packet switching is *not* used as a means of routing information through the network. Point-to-point communications lines are nonswitched.

NORMAL RESPONSE MODE (NRM) - data-transfer scheme in which a primary station in the network may initiate data transfer to a secondary node but a secondary node may only respond to a poll from a primary node.

NOS - see *Network Operation System*.

NOT ACKNOWLEDGE CHARACTER (NAC) - any character used to indicate that transmission of data has been received but errors have been encountered.

NPDA - see *Network Problem Determination Aid*.

NPDU - see *Network Protocol Data Unit*.

NR - see *Number Received*.

NRM - see *Normal Response Mode*.

NRZ - see *Nonreturn to Zero*.

NRZI - see *Nonreturn to Zero Inverted*.

NSAP - see *Network Service Access Point*.

NT - see *Number Transmitted*.

NULL - an ASCII character coded as all zeros used as a filler or to indicate a blank space.

NULL MODEM - any device or cable which acts like a modem and performs the crossover of transmission and reception of data between two devices. Null modems are often used in situations where two AS/400s (or other machines) are in such close proximity that a phone line and conventional modem would not be applicable.

NUMBER RECEIVED (NR) - field used in the transmission frame of some synchronous communications schemes which has the frame number that the receiver should expect to receive next.

NUMBER TRANSMITTTED (NT) - same as *Number Received*, except that the number contained within the frame is that of the frame sequence being transmitted.

NUMBERED FRAMES - an IBM term used in IBM Token-Ring networks to indicate informational segments arranged in numerical order to facilitate accountability.

NYQUIST RATE - a measurement of the theoretical maximum signaling rate of a communications channel.

NYQUIST THEOREM - a theory that states that the maximum signaling rate for a communications channel is twice the channel's bandwidth.

O

OBJECT DISTRIBUTION - an IBM term referring to functions which permit the sending of objects to another user.

OBJECT REQUEST BROKER (ORB) - refers to a software routine used in object-oriented systems which is charged with the task of locating an object in a network and seeing that the operation specified by the object occurs without altering the object's original format.

OCTET - any grouping of eight bits used to represent data. Used in bit synchronous environments.

ODBC - see *Open Database Connectivity.*

ODD PARITY - an error-detection strategy in which the number of bits having a "1" must add up to an odd number; for example, 01010111 contains five "ones", indicating odd parity. See *even parity.*

ODI - see *Open Data-Link Interface.*

OFF HOOK - denoting the active state of a modem, telephone or other communications equipment; in this state, the equipment has answered an incoming call, is transmitting data or is dialing a call.

OFFERED LOAD - refers to the total quantity of messages, bits or packets being presented or offered to a communications device for transmission.

OHM - a unit of measure of the resistance in an electrical circuit (i.e., 72 Ohms). Referred to in Ohm's Law, E=IR, in which resistance in ohms is "R", voltage is "E" and current amps is "I".

OLTP - see *Online Transaction Processing.*

ON-HOOK - the opposite of off-hook; a modem, telephone or other communications device in an inactive state, or when termination of a call occurs.

ONA - see *Open Network Architecture.*

ONLINE DATA TRANSMISSION - any data transmitted from one network node to another under the control of a user.

ONLINE TRANSACTION PROCESSING (OLTP) - any processing environment in which data transmissions are sent in real-time to a processing center or machine which will complete the transaction and return a confirmation to the sender.

OPEN DATA-LINK INTERFACE (ODI) - Novell scheme for the support of multiple protocols without the addition of physical linkage or network boards.

OPEN DATABASE CONNECTIVITY (ODBC) - a middleware standard, created by Microsoft and designed to allow communications and data transfer between heterogeneous database management systems.

OPEN NETWORK ARCHITECTURE (ONA) - refers to any network design in which the emphasis is placed on the networking of heterogeneous systems through standard protocols and structure.

OPEN SHORTEST PATH FIRST (OSPF) - routing scheme use in local area networks incorporating least-cost routing and load balancing.

OPEN SYSTEMS INTERCONNECTION REFERENCE MODEL (OSI) - refers to the seven-layered communications plan for Open Systems Interconnection designed by the ISO. Layers are as follows: 1) Physical; 2) Data Link; 3) Network; 4) Transport; 5) Session; 6) Presentation; 7) Application. Layers two through six are very similar to IBM's System Network Architecture. The purpose for the OSI model is to ensure a framework for the creation of compatible products involving communications between applications.

OPTICAL FIBER - a thin filament of glass, plastic or other material with excellent internal reflection properties. The encoding of information onto the filament may be accomplished via a laser or light-emitting diode (LED). Transmission speeds can approach 20Gbps in some applications.

ORB - see *Object Request Broker.*

ORDERED DELIVERY - refers to the process of reassembling a group of packets into the original form of the transmitted message on X.25 or other packet-switching networks. Due to the nature of packet-switching networks, the message packets may be received out of order from the original message content and ordered delivery ensures their correct assembly.

ORIGINATE MODE - the operating state set up to dial another modem.

OS/2 - an IBM term referring to the operating system for PS/2 computers.

OSI - see *Open Systems Interconnection reference model.*

OSPF - see *Open Shortest Path First.*

OUT-OF-BAND SIGNALING - the use of bandwidth outside of that used for the transfer of information, normally to carry administrative or control information. When used for testing, the term is *out-of-band testing*.

OUTBOUND - as defined for broadband networks, the cable carrying the signal away from the head-end.

OVERHEAD - generally referred to as the bits transmitted in addition to the message text in order to permit the communications protocol to function properly.

P

PABX - see *Private Automatic Branch Exchange.*

PACING - generic term used when two modems are operating at different speeds and an equilibrium of exchange must be established between them.

PACING GROUP - an IBM term used in SNA to denote the quantity of frames which may be sent without an intervening response.

PACKET - general term used to indicate a unit of information of a fixed maximum size, although the actual packet size may be smaller, or variable transmitted over a packet-oriented network.

PACKET ASSEMBLER/DISASSEMBLER (PAD) - refers to a packet-switching network device which assembles character-oriented packets for transmission across the network to the receiving PAD which disassembles the packets.

PACKET BUFFER - section of memory used for the storing of communications packets.

PACKET DISTRIBUTION NETWORK (PDN) - any network, such as X.25, in which the basic unit of data exchange is a packet.

PACKET LEVEL - specific layer of the X.25 standard.

PACKET MODE - terminal device designed to exchange packets of data over a packet-switching network.

PACKET MULTIPLEXING - the use of multiplexing techniques in a packet-oriented network.

PACKET-SWITCHED DATA NETWORK (PSDN) - any network, such as an X.25, in which data communications is achieved via the transmission of packets.

PACKET-SWITCHED EXCHANGE (PSE) - as defined for use in an X.25 network, a PSE is an intermediate network node.

PACKET-SWITCHING NETWORK - any network, such as an X.25 network, in which packets are assembled, transmitted without a predetermined path to the receiver, switched at each node in the network to the required path for delivery to the receiver, and then disassembled upon receipt at the receiver.

PACKETS PER SECOND (PPS) - a measure of throughput of a network expressed in the number of actual packets transmitted in one second of time.

PAD - a device for reducing a signal's strength without injecting noise.

PAD - see *Packet Assembler/Disassembler.*

PAD CHARACTER - any character used to fill up space which would otherwise be occupied by data.

PAGE FRAME NUMBER (PFN) - a number contained within a transmission frame which indicates its session page sequence.

PAGE STRUCTURE - FTP-supported file organization for DEC computers.

PAM - see *Pulse-Amplitude Modulation.*

PAR - see *Positive Acknowledgment Retransmit.*

PARALLEL INTERFACE - generic term for the interface between a device and the multiple input sources inherent with parallel transmissions.

PARALLEL TRANSMISSION - any transmission which sends multiple data bits simultaneously.

PARALLEL-TO-SERIAL CONVERSION - the conversion of parallel data streams into a single, serial data stream.

PARITY - normally associated with odd- or even-parity, it's a method of error detection which uses a parity bit to indicate if the number of 1 bits in a character is odd or even.

PARITY BIT - the bit added to a character to be transmitted which forces the total sum of the 1 bits to be either even or odd.

PARITY CHECK - the validation of the parity bit made by the receiving device to determine whether an error has occurred.

PARITY ERROR - a communications error condition caused by the failure of the parity check to supply the expected result. See *parity* and *parity check.*

PASS WINDOW - another term for bandwidth.

PASS-THROUGH - generic term which denotes the process of accessing one machine via another machine.

PASSIVE HUB - term which denotes a wiring concentration point with no other or "active" functions.

PASSIVE OPEN - refers to the preparations of a TCP/IP server for receiving requests.

PASSIVE RELAY NODES - network nodes with no function other than that of receiving and retransmitting frames of data.

PASSIVE SIDE - refers to the device which sends back the test message in a loopback test.

PASSIVE STAR - modification of the traditional ring topology in which connections are made by means of wiring boxes, implying a star configuration.

PATCH PANEL - panel used to connect devices in a network.

PATH - the route data will take through a network in order to reach its destination. Paths may be temporary, as in virtual paths, or permanent.

PATH CONTROL LAYER SNA - an IBM term referring to the SNA layer charged with establishing logical links between NAUs.

PATH INFORMATION UNIT (PIU) - an IBM term used in SNA to refer to the combination of the TH and BIU information.

PATH LENGTH - refers to the logical, rather than the physical, length of a communications path described in terms of the number of hops between the transmitter and receiver.

PATHNAME - character string used to identify a file as input to a file system.

PBX - see *Private Branch Exchange*.

PCM - see *Pulse-Coded Modulation*.

PCU - see *Programmable Control Unit*.

PDN - see *Packet Distribution Network* and *Public Data Network*.

PDS - see *Premises Distribution System*.

PDU - see *Protocol Data Unit*.

PEAK LOAD - maximum traffic load upon a network.

PEAK TRAFFIC - see *peak load*.

PEAK TRANSACTION LOAD - numerical expression of the number of transactions per second for a network.

PEAK-TO-AVERAGE RATIO - network load ratio calculated by dividing peak load by average load.

PEER LAYERS - refers to the layers in a network which correspond to the sender and the receiver.

PEER PROTOCOL - protocol which defines communications between peer entities.

PEER STATIONS - network nodes which operate at the same level. Neither is slaved to the other.

PEER-TO-PEER RELATIONSHIP - refers to any relationship between two peer nodes or processes in a network.

PENETRATION TAP - special type of cable tap used most often with Ethernet networks.

PERFORMANCE MONITOR - hardware designed specifically to gather data on the performance characteristics of a network.

PERIODIC SIGNALS - signals such as sine waves.

PERIPHERAL NODE CONTROL POINT (PNCP) - an IBM term used in SNA which refers to a peripheral controlling node.

PERMANENT VIRTUAL CIRCUIT (PVC) - 1) a permanent virtual connection between two sites; 2) a CCITT phrase for a dedicated-line type function within an X.25 network.

PERSISTENCE - refers to the probability of a LAN device sending a message when it has the opportunity to do so. A persistence value of 1.0 indicates that the device in question will attempt the transmission 100% of the time, when able.

PERSISTENCE ALGORITHM - algorithm designed for use in contention-based networks which specifies how stations which have caused a network collision must respond.

PERSISTENT CSMA - version of CSMA/CD which has defined rules for reacquiring the communications channel based upon repeated attempts for acquisition.

PFN - see *Page Frame Number.*

PHASE - normally measured in degrees, phase is the attribute of an analog signal which, during a specific period of time, will describe its relative position against a zero baseline.

PHASE JITTER - any unwanted change or alteration in the phase characteristics of a signal.

PHASE MODULATION (PM) - modulation scheme which utilizes changes in the phase of a signal to convey information.

PHASE ROLL - refers to the variations (and echoed-back verification) in the phase of a transmitted signal.

PHASE-SHIFT KEYING (FSK) - modulation method with uses phase modulation--particularly the phase angle of a signal--to indicate 1's and 0's.

PHASE-SHIFT MODULATION (PSM) - another name for *Phase-Shift Keying*.

PHASELOCK LOOP - another term for a phase detector circuit.

PHYSICAL ADDRESS - refers to a unique identifier for a network device.

PHYSICAL CONTROL LAYER - lowest layer of most network models. Charged with managing the physical properties of transmissions including the mechanical and electrical specifications for the network equipment.

PHYSICAL LAYER - see *physical control layer*.

PHYSICAL LAYER SIGNALING (PLS) - refers to the electrical process required to move information onto a communications channel from a transmission interface.

PHYSICAL LINK - any hardware-based communications link.

PHYSICAL MEDIUM ATTACHMENT (PMA) - any device used to physically connect a network node to a network transmission medium.

PHYSICAL PATH - refers to the physical path over which two or more network nodes communicate.

PHYSICAL UNIT (PU) - an IBM term used in SNA to indicate a physical network device and its related resources. PU 1 is normally a nonprogrammable node attached to a PU 4. PU 2 is a peripheral node. PU 4 is a communications controller node and PU 5 is a host node containing a SSCP.

PHYSICAL UNIT CONTROL POINT SNA (PUCP) - an IBM term used in SNA which refers to a network node that controls activity through a subset of SSCP functions but is not an SSCP.

PHYSICAL UNIT TYPE SNA NODE - an IBM term used in SNA to indicate one of the four possible types of PUs. The four are PU 1, PU 2, PU 4 and PU 5.

PHYSICAL-LEVEL RELAY - another term denoting a *repeater*.

PI - see *Protocol Intrepreter*.

PIGGYBACKING - acknowledgment scheme in which the acknowledgment is sent within the message bound for the sender.

PIN - see *Positive-Intrinsic-Negative*.

PING-PONG MULTIPLEXING - a multiplexing scheme also known as *time-compression multiplexing* (TCM), in which small segments of voice messages are sent alternatively in each direction.

PIU - see *Path Information Unit*.

PLAIN OLD TELEPHONE SERVICE (POTS) - the standard public dial telephone network. Ma Bell.

PLASTIC OPTIC FIBER (POF) - plastic-based, optical-fiber transmission media utilizing low-power light to move data up to 100 meters at speeds over 10Mbps.

PLC - see *Power Line Conditioner.*

PLS - see *Physical Layer Signaling.*

PLUG - a generic term used to refer to a male-gender connector.

PM - see *Phase Modulation.*

PM - see *Pulse-Duration Modulation.*

PMA - see *Physical Medium Attachment.*

PMR - see *Poor Man's Routing.*

PNCP - see *Peripheral Node Control Point.*

PODA - see *Priority-Oriented Demand Assignment.*

POF - see *Plastic Optic Fiber.*

POINT-TO-POINT LINE - a communications line between two and only two locations.

POINT-TO-POINT PROTOCOL (PPP) - TCP/IP term describing an Internet protocol used for control of packets across serial data lines.

POLAR SIGNALS - electrical signaling scheme in which positive and negative voltages are used to represent 1's and 0's.

POLL AND SELECT - communications protocol methodology in which a master station polls each slave station, in turn, to transmit data. The master station may also select a specific slave to receive data. Also referred to as *Poll/Call Mode.*

POLL MESSAGE - the actual message sent to a secondary station by a primary station, inviting the transmission of data.

POLL/CALL MODE - see *poll and select.*

POLLED MODE - a communications mode in which a network node has been polled and is responding to the same.

POLLING - the process by which multiple terminals on a multipoint line are successively asked to transmit data.

POLLING DELAY - the duration of time between two different polls of the same device or channel.

POLLING SEQUENCE - refers to the sequence by which polling occurs.

POLYNOMIAL CHECKING - generic term by which error-detection checks are generated, such as a block check character (BCC). Normally, bits in a data block are used in a polynomial function to compute the error-detection character.

POOR MAN'S ROUTING (PMR) - packet network routing scheme which bypasses normal network-layer routing algorithms in favor of source-defined routes to the destination node.

PORT - 1) the point at which a network device interfaces with a communications circuit; 2) a two-octet binary number used in TCP to identify an upper-level user.

PORT ADDRESS - the network-addressable location of a port.

PORT CONTENTION - a situation which occurs when there is more demand for a communications port than can be made available.

PORT NAME - the logical name for a port.

PORT SELECTION - any scheme by which a communications session port is selected.

PORT SELECTOR - any device chartered with selecting a port.

PORT SWITCHING - the process of changing from one port to another transparently.

PORT-SHARING DEVICE - any device created to allow multiple devices to share a common port.

POSITIVE ACKNOWLEDGMENT RETRANSMIT (PAR) - generic name for protocols which send positive messages in response to correct messages and require retransmission of erroneous data.

POSITIVE BIAS - electrical signaling scheme in which positive bit signals are longer than negative bit signals.

POSITIVE-INTRINSIC-NEGATIVE (PIN) - fiber optic-photo detectors.

POSTAMBLE BIT PATTERN - generic term which refers to the pattern of bits transmitted after the main text being sent.

POTS - see *Plain Old Telephone Service.*

POWER - the rate, normally expressed in horsepower or watts, at which work can be performed. Watts equals Volts times Amps (W=V*A).

POWER LINE CONDITIONER (PLC) - official name for a surge-protection strip.

POWER LOSS - the amount of signal strength lost between sender and receiver due to attenuation.

PPM - see *Pulse-Position Modulation.*

PPP - see *Point-to-Point Protocol.*

PPS - see *packets per second.*

PREAMBLE - the piece of a transmitted message which precedes the actual data being sent.

PREMISES DISTRIBUTION SYSTEM (PDS) - cabling scheme for campus area networks or buildings.

PRESENTATION LAYER - in the OSI reference model, the layer chartered with the responsibility for establishing a session, requesting data transfer, negotiating data-transfer syntax, converting data and terminating the session.

PRESENTATION SERVICES LAYER (SNA) - an IBM term used in SNA which provides the same basic functions as the presentation layer of the OSI reference model.

PRESENTATION/APPLICATION PROTOCOLS - those protocols associated with the presentation layer and the application layer of the OSI reference model.

PRIMARY INTERFACE ACCESS ISDN - that level of ISDN service which is comprised of 23 bearer ("B") channels and 1 data ("D") channel. Bandwidth is 1.544Mbps.

PRIMARY STATION - the master station in an unbalanced network. The primary station determines the polling sequence.

PRIMITIVES - as defined for telecommunications, the basic building blocks of signals for the creation of a transfer-control protocol.

PRIORITY-ORIENTED DEMAND ASSIGNMENT (PODA) - communications protocol scheme designed to handle both streaming and burst data. Can be used with voice and data. A reservation methodology is used, as opposed to FIFO.

PRIVATE AUTOMATIC BRANCH EXCHANGE (PABX) - an automated version of a PBX.

PRIVATE BRANCH EXCHANGE (PBX) - switching point chartered with the management of connections and transfers between all internal and external telephone lines.

PRIVATE MANAGEMENT DOMAIN (PRMD) - term used in X.400 message-handling standard to define the domain allocated for a private e-mail system.

PRIVATE NETWORK INTERLINKING SYSTEMS - network scheme for the connection of multiple networks within the same organization.

PRIVATE SINGLE-USE NETWORK - any network designed for a single operation for a specific organization. An example would be ATMs for banks.

PRMD - see *Private Management Domain.*

PROFESSIONAL OFFICE SYSTEM (PROFS) - an IBM term used to refer to its office productivity and e-mail system.

PROFS - see *Professional Office System.*

PROGRAMMABLE CONTROL UNIT (PCU) - any device which is programmable and is used to maintain control over another device.

PROPAGATION - refers to the movement of a signal along a transmission medium.

PROPAGATION DELAY - as stated in the formula T=D/S, where T is time, D is the Distance from transmitter to receiver, and S is the speed of light, propagation delay is the time taken by a signal to travel from the transmitter to the receiver.

PROPAGATION VELOCITY - refers to the speed at which electrical signals are able to travel through a communications medium.

PROTOCOL - generic term referring to a collection of rules and standards implemented to manage and/or execute processes.

PROTOCOL CONVERTER - any device (hardware- or software-based) which receives an incoming protocol stream, remaps it into a different protocol stream and then retransmits it.

PROTOCOL DATA UNIT (PDU) - protocol-managed exchange of data between network nodes.

PROTOCOL FAMILY - any group of communications protocols making use of the same addressing scheme.

PROTOCOL FILE TRANSFER - any of the protocols, normally located at the application layer of a network reference model, charged with internodal data file transfer.

PROTOCOL FILTERING - facility often found in bridges, routers and brouters for eliminating (filtering) certain protocol transmissions.

PROTOCOL INTERPRETER (PI) - an entity which performs FTP functions.

PROTOCOL STACK - see *protocol suite*.

PROTOCOL SUITE - refers to a set of protocols which are similar or related in function.

PSDN - see *Packet-Switched Data Network*.

PSE - see *Packet-Switched Exchange*.

PSEUDO-RANDOM BIT PATTERNS - network facilities test pattern composed of either 511 or 2,047 bits which include all possible bit sequences.

PSK - see *Phase-Shift Keying*.

PSM - see *Phase-Shift Modulation*.

PSTN - see *Public Switched Telephone Network*.

PU - see *Physical Unit*.

PU-TO-PU SESSION SNA - an IBM term referring to a network session between two PUs, usually controlled by an SSCP.

PUBLIC DATA NETWORK (PDN) - any network under government supervision or control which is available for public usage.

PUBLIC LINES - telephone lines regulated by the FCC.

PUBLIC SWITCHED TELEPHONE NETWORK (PSTN) - a hierarchical network supplying switched communications circuits to subscribers.

PUCP - see *Physical Unit Control Point SNA*.

PULSE-AMPLITUDE MODULATION (PAM) - scheme for modulation which incorporates pulse-to-amplitude signaling.

PULSE-CODED MODULATION (PCM) - modulation scheme in which the magnitude of a signal's sample is coded as a digital signal.

PULSE-DURATION MODULATION (PDM) - modulation scheme in which data is encoded based on the duration of a pulse, with the difference in pulses indicating 1's and 0's.

PULSE-POSITION MODULATION (PPM) - modulation scheme in which the position of a pulse during the bit time will determine the status of 1's and 0's.

PULSE-WIDTH MODULATION (PWM) - modulation scheme in which the breadth of a pulse is used to convey 1's and 0's. Also known as *Pulse-Duration Modulation*.

PUNCH-DOWN BLOCK - wiring panel at which wires from individual devices are terminated and connected to backbone, trunk or other sources.

PUSH SERVICE - TCP service allowing an application to specify that some data should be delivered on a priority basis.

PVC - see *Permanent Virtual Circuit.*

PWM - see *Pulse-Width Modulation.*

Q

Q.921 - an ISO-based, data-link protocol used in ISDN networks.

Q.931 - an ISO-based, network-layer protocol used in ISDN networks.

QAM - see *Quadrature Amplitude Modulation.*

QLLC - see *Qualified Logical Link Control.*

QPSK - see *Quadrature Phase-Shift Keying.*

QTAM - see *Queued Telecommunications Access Method.*

QUADBIT - refers to the process of four bits encoded on one signal.

QUADRATURE AMPLITUDE MODULATION (QAM) - a modulation technique in which multiple bits are encoded on a single signal through a combination of phase and amplitude changes.

QUADRATURE PHASE-SHIFT KEYING (QPSK) - modulation technique wherein four separate phase shifts are used to encode two bits of information on a signal.

QUALIFIED LOGICAL LINK CONTROL (QLLC) - an IBM phrase referring to the ability of SDLC data streams to be carried over an X.25 packet switching network as directed by ACF/NCP.

QUANTIZATION - refers to the process by which the continuous disposition of values contained within an input signal is segmented into subranges after having a discrete value assigned to each subrange value.

QUANTIZATION ERROR - a measure of the amount of error than can be expected when an analog waveform is digitized into quantum intervals. See *quantizing noise.*

QUANTIZING NOISE - the actual error introduced when an analog signal is quantized. See *quantizing error.*

QUARANTINE SERVICE - a form of security for incoming communication messages in which all the messages of a communication are collected in a buffer *before* the first message is processed.

QUEUED TELECOMMUNICATIONS ACCESS METHOD (QTAM) - an IBM phrase referring to an access methodology prevalent before the advent of virtual systems, that performed I/O for telecommunications applications.

QUEUING - describes the process of placing incoming items waiting for service into a line or list.

QUEUING DELAYS - a measure of the amount of time a message/frame must wait for transmission as a function of queuing. The queuing rules used for selection of transaction servicing may include First-In, First-Out (FIFO), Random, Last-In First-Out (LIFO), or via a priority scheme. See *queuing*.

QUEUING NETWORKS - a network composed of a series of queues at each node within the network.

QUIESCE/SHUTDOWN - the termination (either temporary or permanent) of data flow between two points in a network.

QUIESCENT STATE - a state of no data transmission. See *Quiesce/Shutdown*.

QUIESCING - the stopping of the flow of data within a network.

R

RADIO FREQUENCY (RF) - Electromagnetic waves operating between 10KHz and 3MHz propagated in free space.

RADIO FREQUENCY INTERFERENCE (RFI) - transmitted radio waves which may interfere with the operation of electronic devices.

RANDOM ROUTING - a network routing scheme in which the next routing link is selected at random from all possible links in an effort to prevent network congestion and delays.

RANDOM-ACCESS TECHNIQUES - access schemes which provide multiple devices with access to a shared channel. In the event of a collision, all stations wait a random amount of time and then attempt access again.

RARP - see *Reverse Address Resolution Protocol.*

RAS - an IBM term referring to the "reliability and serviceability" of equipment-maintenance goals.

RCC - see *Routing Control Center.*

RD - see *Receive Data.*

RDC - see *Remote Data Concentrator.*

REAL-TIME - the minimum time elapsed between an event and a response to that event.

REASSEMBLY - the process of reconstructing a complete message from a series of segmented packets.

REASSEMBLY DEADLOCK - a condition occurring within packet-switching networks in which a packet assembler/disassembler (PAD) is waiting for a required packet to arrive to complete a message and the sending site is unaware of the missing packet.

RECEIVE DATA (RD) - the EIA RS-232 connection over which serial devices receive data. The reception line for incoming data in the 25-pin RS-232 standard is pin 3. In the 9-pin PC interface, it's pin 2.

RECEIVE WINDOW - a numerical set describing the range of sequence numbers which may be transmitted at a specific time during a connection.

RECEIVER ISOLATION - a term used to describe the loss of signal strength between any two receivers that are connected on a cable system.

RECONFIGURATION - the process of creating a new network configuration based upon a previous network configuration to allow for the addition or loss of network components or the redesign of the network to optimize performance.

RECOVERY - the process of returning to an operational state following a system failure or other catastrophic event.

REDUNDANCY CHECKING - an error-checking technique in which the bits of a message are used to create an extra bit or character that is sent as part of the original message to ensure the accuracy of the received message. See *Vertical Redundancy Check* and *Longitudinal Redundancy Check*.

REFERENCE MODEL FOR OPEN SYSTEMS INTERCONNECTION - see *OSI reference model*.

REFLECTIONS - also known as echoes, a secondary signal created through the collision of a transmitted signal and an object in its path, cable impedance mismatches, or cable irregularities.

REGENERATIVE REPEATER - any of the family of devices which regenerates digital signals by retiming, reshaping and retransmitting the received digital signal.

REGIME - a communications protocol term referring to any collection of related services, processes or operations.

REGISTER INSERTION - a type of ring in which the device interface has shift registers which can increase the total number of bits that the ring can contain at any one time.

RELAY POINTS - any network point at which information is relayed (switched) to other network circuits.

RELEASE CONTROL - a term for describing the orderly termination of a connection and return of the released network resources to the network control program (NCP).

RELIABLE TRANSFER SERVICE (RTS) - a software service available in X.400 electronic mail networks to validate the selection of the most efficient route for a message.

REM - see *Ring Error Monitor*.

REMOTE BATCH PROCESSING - a data-processing method in which the data required for processing is gathered together at a remote location and then forwarded to a computer for final processing.

REMOTE DATA CONCENTRATOR (RDC) - a data concentrator remotely located from the network nodes for which the concentration is being executed.

REMOTE DISTRIBUTED PROCESSING - the ability to have data-processing functions executed at remote (distributed) locations across a network.

REMOTE FILE SHARING (RFS) - having the ability for network users to access remote data files located at remote locations across a network.

REMOTE JOB ENTRY (RJE) - an IBM term referring to software created to process the input, scheduling and output of work submitted, via batch form, from a remote terminal. Current version is called *Job Entry Subsystem* (JES).

REMOTE MANAGEMENT FACILITY (RMF) - a remote network control point not physically located at the primary network control center (NCC).

REMOTE NETWORK MONITOR (RMON) - any of the devices designed to collect data on network traffic patterns.

REMOTE NETWORK MONITORING (RMON) - refers to a protocol for monitoring remote networks.

REMOTE OPERATIONS SERVICE ELEMENT (ROSE) - an object providing the ability to start, stop and control remote operations. Described within the application layer of protocol stacks.

REMOTE PROCEDURE CALL (RPC) - a communications protocol designed to permit a given application to "call" a routine that will execute at the server and then have the server return the results of the call to the calling application.

REMOTE SPOOLING COMMUNICATIONS SUBSYSTEM (RSCS) - an IBM term referring to a Job Entry Subsystem used with VM machines.

REMOTE TELECOMMUNICATIONS ACCESS METHOD (RTAM) - an IBM term referring to a mainframe subsystem processing applications access and routing within a network.

REMOTE TERMINAL EMULATION (RTE) - system software used to generate test traffic by emulating the transmissions from multiple terminals.

REMOVE - a networking term referring to the stopping of an adapter from participation in data exchange.

REPEATER - any of the family of digital devices designed to lengthen the span of a local area network.

REPLICATED FILES - a type of distributed file processing wherein required files are duplicated at various points within a network.

REQUEST FOR INITIALIZATION (RQI) - an IBM term for an SDLC frame control field.

REQUEST ON LINE (ROL) - an IBM term referring to an SDLC frame control field.

REQUEST TO SEND (RTS) - an RS-232 signal used as a "handshake" to place a modem in a ready state for transmission of data. Also used in half-duplex communications to indicate and control the direction of transmission. In the 25-pin RS-232 interface, RTS is pin 4. In the 9-pin PC interface, it's pin 7.

REQUEST/RESPONSE HEADER (RH) - an IBM term; in SNA, the three-byte RH is added to the RU by the transaction control layer, creating a Basic Information Unit (BIU) to be passed to the path control layer.

REQUEST/RESPONSE UNIT (RU) - an IBM term used to describe units of information passing between network-addressable units (NAUs). See *Request/Response Header*.

REQUESTS FOR COMMENTS (RFCs) - the documentation set containing, among other things, the specifics of Internet protocol and other germane issues.

REROUTING - the alteration of an established route between two devices on a network due to network congestion, component failure or other circumstances.

RES - Remote Entry Services. See *JES*.

RESERVATION ACCESS - the assignment of a time slice in a noncontention system to a requesting location by a controlling location.

RESERVATION PROTOCOL - a communications protocol that grants temporary, but exclusive, use of a portion of the network to participating stations.

RESIDUAL ERROR RATE - a measurement of the communications errors which have passed unchecked to a communications destination.

RESOLVER - any of a group of software products which allows access to the Domain Name System database.

RESOURCE NAME - a name assigned to a line, controller or other network device.

RESOURCE-SHARING NETWORKS - communications networks designed to facilitate the sharing of network resources due to costing or other constraints.

RESPONSE TIME - elapsed time between the completion of a request (e.g., pressing the Help key on the AS/400) and the appearance of the response.

RESPONSE TIME ESTIMATE (RTE) - a calculated approximation of estimated response time. See *response time*.

RETRANSMISSION TIME-OUT - a value specified within TCP indicating the duration of time allowed to pass without receiving an ACK, after which TCP will retransmit a segment.

RETRY LIMIT/COUNT - the process of reattempting a failed task or event until a limit or count of retries is reached.

RETURN BAND - a one-way channel within frequency-division multiplexers assigned the task of transmitting remote device responses to a central control device.

RETURN CODE - a value which supplies the result of an adapter action.

RETURN LOSS - a decibel measurement of the reflective properties of a component.

RETURN PATH - see *Reverse Direction*.

RETURN TO ZERO (RZ) - signaling scheme in which a one-bit pulse does not achieve its full bit time due to the necessity of the pulse to return to a zero state before or after the bit time.

REVERSE ADDRESS RESOLUTION PROTOCOL (RARP) - a communications protocol designed to permit a computer to identify its IP address by means of a broadcast request on the network.

REVERSE CHANNEL - a line turnaround mechanism used in low-speed, half-duplex communications.

REVERSE CHARGING - refers to the capacity of an X.25 network DTE to request that the cost of a communications session be allocated to the target DTE.

REVERSE DIRECTION - in a broadband network cable system, the direction of a signal toward the head-end.

REVERSE INTERRUPT (RVI) - bisync control message functioning as both an ACK and as an indication to the sender to stop sending because the receiver is in possession of a high-priority message.

RF - see *Radio Frequency*.

RF MODEM - a modem designed to transmit analog signals onto a wire between communications devices.

RFCs - see *Requests for Comments*.

RFI - see *Radio Frequency Interference*.

RFS - see *Remote File Sharing*.

RH - see *Request/Response Header*.

RI - see *Ring Indicator*.

RIBBON CABLE - a wide, flat, multiconductor cable used in RS-232 connections between DTEs and DCEs.

RING ERROR MONITOR (REM) - a facility within a single token-ring network charged with the collection of error information and fault isolation/correction.

RING IN - the input or receive receptacle on an IBM multistation access unit (MAU).

RING INDICATOR (RI) - a line in the EIA RS-232 interface used to indicate to a computer or terminal device that the telephone is ringing. In the 25-pin RS-232 interface, RI is pin 22; in the 9-pin PC interface, it's pin 9.

RING NETWORK - a network design similar to a loop network. Access to the ring is controlled via a permission code and each node is connected to two adjacent nodes with repeaters, forming a closed loop or "ring".

RING OUT - the output or transmit receptacle on an IBM multistation access unit (MAU).

RING SEQUENCE - an IBM term referring to the physical connection order of Token-Ring network components.

RING STATUS - an IBM term referring to the condition of a Token-Ring network.

RINGER EQUIVALENCE - a Federal Communications Commission (FCC) electrical standard applied to modem equipment designed to be connected to the public telephone system.

RIP - see *Routing Information Protocol*.

RJ45 - variation of RJll jack allowing a wider variety of signal paths to be accommodated.

RJ48 - the AT&T telephone jack used in ISDN applications.

RJE - see *Remote Job Entry*.

RJllC - a single-line telephone jack used to connect modems and telephones to telephone systems.

RMF - see *Remote Management Facility*.

RMON - see *Remote Network Monitor* and *Remote Network Monitoring*.

ROL - see *Request On Line*.

ROLL-CALL POLLING - a polling scheme in which secondary stations are polled by the master station as dictated by their placement on a polling list.

ROLL-OFF - term used to describe the smoothing of a signal's normally sharp transitions or peaks.

ROOT BRIDGE - the bridge allocated the top spot in a multi-bridge local area network.

ROSE - see *Remote Operations Service Element*.

ROUND-TRIP TIME (RTT) - a measurement of the duration of time between the transmission of a TCP segment and the receipt of its acknowledgment (ACK).

ROUTE - the path communications information takes during its transmission from one network point to another.

ROUTER - a network node responsible for the movement of messages/frames from one network station to another network station on another network.

ROUTING - the process of selecting the direction of transmitted packets.

ROUTING CONTROL CENTER (RCC) - the device and/or routing software which performs centralized routing for an entire network.

ROUTING INFORMATION PROTOCOL (RIP) - communications protocol employing the Bellman-Ford algorithm to monitor the route between source and destination nodes through the use of a "hop" count.

ROUTING NETWORK - a communications network in which the routing of data packets is founded on the addressing information located within the packet. Dynamic routing is used to move the packets from node to node.

RPC - see *Remote Procedure Call*.

RQI - see *Request for Initialization*.

RS-232 - EIA electrical interface standard describing the manufacture of serial data communications equipment.

RS-243 - EIA electrical interface standard describing the characteristics of Unbalanced voltage digital interface circuits.

RS-422 - EIA electrical interface standard which describes the characteristics of balanced voltage digital interface circuits.

RS-449 - EIA electrical interface standard describing the characteristics of 37-pin and 9-pin general-purpose interfaces used with data terminal and data circuit-terminating equipment which utilize serial binary data interchange.

RS/6000 - IBM's line of RISC-based engineering workstations and servers, first introduced in 1990.

RSCS - see *Remote Spooling Communications Subsystem*.

RTAM - see *Remote Telecommunications Access Method*.

RTE - see *Remote Terminal Emulation* and *Response Time Estimate*.

RTS - see *Request to Send* and *Reliable Transfer Service*.

RTT - see *Round-Trip Time*.

RU - see *Request/Response Unit*.

RVI - see *Reverse Interrupt*.

RZ - see *Return to Zero*.

S

S/N - see *Signal-to-Noise ratio.*

SAA - see *System Application Architecture.*

SABM - see *Set Asynchronous Balanced Mode.*

SABME - see *Set Asynchronous Balanced Mode Extended.*

SAP - see *Service Access Point.*

SATELLITE - for our purposes, a man-made device which orbits the earth and is used for communications transmission and reception.

SATELLITE CARRIERS - refers to companies or organizations who supply satellite communications services.

SATELLITE CHANNELS - communication channels used in satellite data transmission. Normally microwave in nature, they are used for the uplink (to the satellite) and downlink (from the satellite) and often use the 4/6GHz or 12/14GHz frequency bands.

SATELLITE DELAY COMPENSATION UNIT - methodologies and equipment used in satellite communications to offset the propagation delay associated with the transmission of data through a satellite link. This delay is caused by the geosynchronous orbit of satellites.

SATELLITE-SWITCHED TIME-DIVISION MULTIPLE ACCESS (SS/TDMA) - refers to a form of time-division multiplexing in which channel assignments are manipulated to allow multiple access to a common satellite channel.

SBT - see *Six-Bit Transcode.*

SCB - see *String Control Byte.*

SCRAMBLER - a device used to jumble a transmitted signal so that only a location with a matching device can unjumble it into its original state.

SCSI - see *Small Computer System Interface.*

SDLC - see *Synchronous Data Link Control.*

SDM - see *Subrate Data Multiplexer* and *Space-Division Multiplexing.*

SDN - see *Software-Defined Network*.

SDU - see *Service Data Unit*.

SECONDARY CHANNEL - a communications channel utilized in the transmission of control information relating to a main or primary channel's transmission.

SECONDARY LOGICAL UNIT (SLU) - a term normally referring to an LU type 1, 2, 3, 4 or 7 terminal, which is subordinate to a primary logical unit.

SECONDARY STATION - a slave station or tributary station in an unbalanced or normal response mode type of network. Secondary stations are incapable of starting data transfer and must be polled by a primary or master station.

SEGMENT - refers to that portion of an IBM Token-Ring network which may contain cables, components and lobes.

SEGMENTATION - the partitioning of a network into segments, or the division of a long message into smaller pieces.

SELECT - a subset of polling, this is the method by which a master or primary station requests authorization from a secondary station to send data to it.

SELECTIVE REJECT ARQ PROTOCOL - refers to a protocol scheme in which receiving stations can request a retransmission of a certain block(s) out of the sequence of blocks already transmitted to it.

SELECTIVE REPEAT ARQ - refers to that portion of a continuous ARQ protocol in which the receiver is able to request the retransmission of a specific block of data which was in error.

SELF-CHECKING CODE - a phrase referring to an error-detection scheme in which the code used has redundant bits capable of acting in a self-checking, error-detection mode.

SELF-HEALING RING - a networking scheme utilizing two concentric network rings which carry data in opposite directions from each other. Upon detection of a network break or failure, the network will automatically allow the nodes closest to the break to bridge to the other ring, thus forming a new ring and continuing the flow of data uninterrupted.

SEMAPHORES - network flags arranged to ensure that two processes don't attempt to access the same resource at the same time.

SEQUENCE CHECKS - refers to the checks made within a network which will ensure the proper arrival sequence of messages sent.

SEQUENCE NUMBER - a 32-bit field used in a TCP header.

SEQUENCED PACKET EXCHANGE (SPX) - a Novell-designed packet protocol used for serialization operations, file transfer and file access in NetWare-based networks.

SEQUENCED PACKET PROTOCOL (SPP) - a Banyan-designed packet protocol used for serialization, file transfer and file access in VINES-based networks.

SEQUENCING - refers to the process of allocating sequence numbers to messages in order to allow for correct message ordering and/or error-detection schemes.

SERIAL LINE INTERNET PROTOCOL (SLIP) - refers to a point-to-point link often used in TCP/IP network for the connection of two devices on a serial line.

SERIAL TRANSMISSION - as opposed to parallel transmission, serial transmission involves the movement of successive bits over a communications line.

SERIES - in an electrical context, a group of devices set in a sequential arrangement.

SERVER - a local area network term for a device which receives and manages requests for specialized services for other devices also attached to the network (e.g., print server, communication server, SAA server).

SERVER MESSAGE BLOCK (SMB) - an IBM term referring to the protocol for the usage of a distributed file system within a local area network.

SERVER/REQUESTER PROGRAM INTERFACE (SRPI) - an IBM term used to indicate the applications programming interface (API) used with communications between IBM's Enhanced Communications Facility (ECF) and LU type 2.

SERVICE ACCESS POINT (SAP) - a point, referred to by address, in a network at which two protocol layers meet.

SERVICE DATA UNIT (SDU) - refers to a data area utilized in OSI-oriented systems for user-specific data.

SERVICE PROVIDERS - any vendor which provides communication services.

SERVICES - the specific functions supplied by service providers.

SESSION - 1) an IBM term referring to the communications between two network-addressable units (NAUs); 2) any connection between two stations on a network or system.

SESSION CONTROL - layered network services that control, start and stop sessions between stations in a network.

SESSION LAYER - as viewed from the OSI reference model, any layer of a network scheme that corresponds with the fifth layer of the reference model, providing for the establishment, termination and management of application-layer entity network sessions.

SESSION PROTOCOL DATA UNIT (SPDU) - refers to any session protocol entity data unit created to manipulate network services.

SESSION PROTOCOL MACHINE (SPM) - as viewed from the OSI reference model, the limited-state model outlining the implementation of a session-layer protocol.

SESSION RECOVERY UNIT - describes the unit whose task is to recover from a session interruption or loss of synchronization.

SET ASYNCHRONOUS BALANCED MODE (SABM) - an IBM term used to establish a data link connection for asymmetric communications.

SET ASYNCHRONOUS BALANCED MODE EXTENDED (SABME) - extended version of SABM.

SET NORMAL RESPONSE MODE (SNRM) - an IBM term used to indicate a control field in an SDLC frame.

SG - see *Signal Ground.*

SHIELDED TWISTED-PAIR (STP) - a wire similar to unshielded twisted-pair except that it possesses a form of shielding from unwanted electromagnetic noise and/or signal loss.

SHIELDING - any protective covering that reduces or eliminates electromagnetic and/or radio frequency interference.

SHIFT IN - communications control word used to signal a return to the default meaning of the data codes to follow.

SHIFT OUT - communications control word used to signal an alternative meaning to the data codes to follow.

SHIFT REGISTERS - encoders/decoders used in data communications in which the bits in each register are moved ("shifted") to the next register.

SHM - see *Short-Hold Mode.*

SHORT-HAUL MODEM - a modem designed to condition a digital signal for transmission over a DC continuous private line at ranges of up to 20 miles and speeds generally through 19,200bps.

SHORT-HOLD MODE (SHM) - an IBM term used in SNA networks to indicate a type of X.21 communications mode in which a terminal may connect to the X.21 network for a short peroid while maintaining logical SNA connection.

SIDE INFORMATION - in the AS/400 world, a combination of directory services data and data from the OSI subsystem's information base.

SIDEBANDS - those frequencies located on the upper and lower sides of a carrier frequency.

SIGNAL - a pulsed or changing physical quantity used to represent data. Digital signals are discrete and analog signals are continuous.

SIGNAL CONVERSION - the changing of a signal type from one form to another. What modems do when converting digital signals to analog and vice versa.

SIGNAL GENERATOR - a family of test devices used for the generation of signals. Control is maintained over the signal's waveform, frequency, amplitude and other factors.

SIGNAL GROUND (SG) - the physical point at which a signal is attached to an electrical ground. Also a lead on the RS-232 interface. In the 25-pin RS-232C standard, it's pin 7; on the 9-pin PC interface, it's pin 5.

SIGNAL LEVEL - refers to the root-mean-square (RMS) voltage as sampled during the peak of a radio frequency signal.

SIGNAL LOSS - the measurement of the reduction in power of a signal transmitted between two points; also called *attenuation*.

SIGNAL SPECTRUM - the frequency span of a signal.

SIGNAL-TO-NOISE RATIO (S/N) - as expressed in decibels, this is the ratio or relationship of the the power of a signal and the power of the noise inherent in the transmission of the signal.

SIGNALING SYSTEM 7 (SS7) - refers to the international specification agreements for the design of a common channel signaling (CCS) scheme which has the capability of supporting, among others, ISDN.

SIGNALING SYSTEM MODEM STANDARDS - standards such as the CCITT's "V" series, which have been written to establish a level playing field for modem manufacturers and to allow modems from different firms to communicate with each other.

SIGNALING TERMINAL EXCHANGE (STE) - refers to the family of devices used in the connection of X.25 networks.

SIMPLE MAIL TRANSFER PROTOCOL (SMTP) - an electronic mail protocol designed for use within TCP networks and utilizing a portion of the application layer of TCP to do so.

SIMPLE NETWORK MANAGEMENT PROTOCOL (SNMP) - a network management protocol designed for use on Internet to manage network devices from different vendors.

SIMPLEX CIRCUIT - a communications circuit capable of one-way data transfer only.

SIMPLEX TRANSMISSION - a communications transmission in which one-way only signals are transmitted. Watching television is an example of a simplex transmission.

SINE WAVE - a type of waveform having the following characteristics: it's continuously varying and has amplitude, phase and frequency.

SINGING - the characteristic tonal responses of a modem trying to synchronize itself with another modem.

SINGLE PORT SHARING - an IBM term referring to the port-sharing capabilities of DTEs involved in a short-hold mode operation.

SINGLE SESSION - a term referring to the communications nature of a device, specifically to its ability to have only one host session at a time.

SINGLE SIDEBAND (SSB) - describes the phenomenon of the production of upper and lower frequency ban adjacent ro a carrier frequency as created by the modulation process.

SINGLE THREADING - refers to a system or process in which one transaction is carried through to completion before another can begin.

SINGLE-CHANNEL BROADBAND - refers to an analog transmission mode in which the entire bandwidth is devoted to one channel and not split among many different channels.

SINGLE-NODE NETWORK - a network design scheme based around a single circuit-switched node.

SINGLE-SIDEBAND SUPPRESSED CARRIER (SSBSC) - a transmission communications scheme which utilizes only one sideband and no carrier wave.

SINGLE-STATION - a term used to refer to a terminal emulation product's ability to have a host connection other than through a gateway.

SINGLE-SYSTEM ELECTRONIC MAIL - a type of electronic mail system in which only the users connected to the network are able to send and receive mail.

SIX-BIT TRANSCODE (SBT) - an IBM term denoting a six-bit character code designed for use with RJE.

SLIP - see *Serial Line Internet Protocol*.

SLOPE - a term used in broadband networking to indicate the difference between the highest and lowest frequency in a cable system.

SLU - see *Secondary Logical Unit*.

SMALL COMPUTER SYSTEM INTERFACE (SCSI) - pronounced "skuzzy", an ANSI standard parallel, multimaster I/O bus used to interface microcomputers and peripheral devices. SCSI interfaces have nine data lines and nine control signals.

SMART MODEM - a preprogrammed or programmable modem which includes user-friendly features such as auto-speed fallback, callback and other such "adaptive" features.

SMB - see *Server Message Block* and *System Message Block*.

SMOOTHED DEVIATION - refers to the measured deviation quantity of the smoothed round-trip time used for the calculation of TCP retransmission time-outs.

SMOOTHED ROUND-TRIP TIME (SRTT) - a value used in the calculation of TCP time-outs, it is an estimate of the round-trip time for a transmission segment and its associated ACK.

SMTP - see *Simple Mail Transfer Protocol*.

SNA - see *System Network Architecture*.

SNADS - see *System Network Architecture Distribution Services*.

SNBU - see *Switched Network Backup*.

SNMP - see *Simple Network Management Protocol*.

SNRM - see *Set Normal Response Mode*.

SNUF - see *System Network Architecture Upline Facility*.

SOCKET ADDRESS - the full address of a TCP/IP entity comprised of the 32-bit network address in conjunction with the 16-bit port number.

SOFTWARE-DEFINED NETWORK (SDN) - refers to a network scheme which utilizes a software-driven "virtual network" which may be defined via software and then dynamically reconfigured, thus eliminating the problems associated with fixed-hardware connections.

SOH - see *Start of Header*.

SOM - see *Start of Message*.

SONET - see *Synchronous Optical Network*.

SOURCE ROUTING - a routing scheme in which the permissible routes in a network are kept at each node in the network.

SOURCE ROUTING PROTOCOL - an IBM term referring to the IBM Token-Ring routing protocol in which source stations analyze the network's available bridges to determine the available paths to the destination.

SOURCE ROUTING TRANSPARENT (SRT) - routing scheme in which transparent bridging is the determining factor as to whether or not to forward frames.

SOURCE SERVICE ACCESS POINT (SSAP) - as used in the 802.3 protocol, the concatenation of the local address with the service access point (source) address from the logical link control layer.

SPACE - in data communications, a space is normally equal to a binary zero.

SPACE ASYNCHRONOUS - refers to the start bit in asynchronous communications used to denote the beginning of the transmission of a character.

SPACE-DIVISION MULTIPLEXING (SDM) - multiplexing scheme which combines multiple separate physical circuits into one large cable, with each separate cable carrying its own data.

SPANNING TREE - a form of tree network in which the network contains a root node and one path which connects all other nodes.

SPDU - see *Session Protocol Data Unit*.

SPIKE NOISE - signal noise caused by random pulses of electricity.

SPIRAL REDUNDANCY CHECKING - a type of longitudinal error-checking in which the bit positions verified by the parity bit are offset by one or more positions from one character to the next.

SPLITTER - a device designed to divide a signal into two or more signals.

SPM - see *Session Protocol Machine*.

SPP - see *Sequenced Packet Protocol*.

SPREAD SPECTRUM - a type of transmission in which wide sections of the bandwidth spectrum are utilized. Examples might include television and radio.

SPX - see *Sequenced Packet Exchange*.

SQUARE WAVE - type of waveform which has two discrete states in which to represent a digital signal.

SRCT - see *Start of Record Control Byte*.

SRPI - see *Server/Requester Program Interface*.

SRT - see *Source Routing Transparent*.

SRTT - see *Smoothed Round-Trip Time*.

SS/TDMA - see *Satellite-Switched Time-Division Multiple Access.*

SS7 - see *Signaling System 7.*

SSAP - see *Source Service Access Point.*

SSB - see *Single Sideband.*

SSBSC - see *Single Sideband Suppressed Carrier.*

SSCP - see *System Service Control Point.*

STANDARDS - refers to the formal formats, procedures and design representations which allow hardware and/or software portability, interoperability and reliability across systems.

STAR NETWORK - network design in which all nodes of the network are connected to a central host.

STAR WIRING - wiring scheme in which all network cables flow from a central point.

START OF HEADER (SOH) - transmission control character used to indicate the start of the header part of a message.

START OF MESSAGE (SOM) - communications control character used to identify the message start in byte-oriented protocols.

START OF RECORD CONTROL BYTE (SRCT) - an IBM term used to indicate the start of a record in IBM's multileaving compression methodology.

START OF TEXT (STX) - communications control character used to indicate that the following data is the text of the message. Used in bisync communications.

START SEQUENCE - bit sequence utilized in the establishment of synchronization between sending and receiving stations.

START/STOP SYNCHRONIZATION - see *asynchronous.*

START/STOP TRANSMISSION - see *asynchronous.*

STATION - refers to any device on a network capable of sending and/or receiving data.

STATISTICAL MULTIPLEXER (STATMUX) - multiplexer which uses statistical time-division multiplexing to transfer data. See *statistical time-division multiplexing.*

STATISTICAL TIME-DIVISION MULTIPLEXING (STDM) - multiplexing scheme in which multiple low-speed device elements are dynamically allocated on a single high-speed communications link. The time "slots" for the high-speed channel are not preallocated but are assigned, normally on a first-come, first-serve basis from the lower speed devices.

STATMUX - see *Statistical Multiplexer*.

STE - see *Signaling Terminal Exchange*.

STOP BIT - communications control character used to indicate the end of a string of bits in an asynchronous communications transmission.

STOP-N-WAIT ARQ - communications transmission protocol in which the sender waits until the receipt of the last transmission before sending another.

STORE-AND-FORWARD - communications scheme in which messages are stored at one location and forwarded to a receiver at a later time.

STP - see *Shielded Twisted-Pair*.

STRAIGHT-THROUGH PINNING - RS-232 and RS-422 scheme that mates DTE to DCE, pin for pin.

STRING CONTROL BYTE (SCB) - an IBM term denoting a byte used in their multileaving data-compression protocol that indicates the length and interpretation of the character string to follow.

STX - see *Start of Text*.

SUBAREA - an IBM term referring to a group of addressable elements with the same subarea identification located within an SNA network.

SUBAREA NODES - an IBM term referring to a node within an SNA domain which controls all the resources in the domain.

SUBCARRIER - refers to a given frequency below that of the carrier.

SUBLAN - see Zero-Slot LAN.

SUBNET ADDRESS - a network address created from a group of bits in the local IP address, and used to indicate a specific local or wide area network.

SUBNETWORK - any logically separate portion of a network.

SUBRATE DATA MULTIPLEXER (SDM) - refers to that family of multiplexers which utilizes data transfer rates less than that used for voice-grade communications (less than 4KHz). 2,400, 4,800 and 9,600bps are all subrate.

SUPERFRAME - a phrase used in Tl multiplexers to denote the 12-frame sequence of data.

SUPERVISORY FRAMES - data transmission control frames used to convey network management and control data.

SVC - see *Switched Virtual Circuit*.

SWITCH - any device capable of a switching function.

SWITCHED CONNECTION - a communications connection between two locations by means of one or more switching nodes.

SWITCHED LINE - any communications line which must be dialed up or otherwise attached to a switch in order to achieve a communications link.

SWITCHED NETWORK BACKUP (SNBU) - a feature of some modems which allows, upon selection, a nonswitched line to be used as a switched line and vice versa.

SWITCHED VIRTUAL CIRCUIT (SVC) - refers to a virtual circuit established between stations for the duration of the session only.

SWITCHED-CARRIER SYSTEM - type of system used in analog multipoint communications in which each modem located at a station utilizes a different frequency and in which the controlling station changes frequency in order to match those of the devices it needs to contact.

SYMMETRIC PROTOCOL - any protocol which results in a connection between peers.

SYN - see *Synchronous Idle*.

SYNCHRONIZATION - the process of keeping the timing between stations coordinated.

SYNCHRONIZATION COMMUNICATIONS ADAPTER - an IBM term referring to a hardware interface used in the support of synchronous communications.

SYNCHRONIZATION POINTS - refers to any point at which synchronization must be kept to ensure the successful completion of a task or function.

SYNCHRONIZATION SEQUENCE - any method used to achieve synchronization.

SYNCHRONOUS DATA LINK CONTROL (SDLC) - an IBM term referring to its link-controlled, bit-oriented protocol composed of different frames. SDLC is code-independent and transparent to data being handled, and includes path control.

SYNCHRONOUS IDLE (SYN) - control character used in block transmission protocols to allow the sending and receiving stations to achieve synchronization. Also used as fill characters during idle line time; SYN value in EBCDIC is (00110010) and in ASCII is (00010110).

SYNCHRONOUS OPTICAL NETWORK (SONET) - optical-based, high-speed network used as part of the public telephone system.

SYSTEM APPLICATION ARCHITECTURE (SAA) - an IBM term referring to the formats and protocols designed to create a consistent environment and common programming interfaces across multiple systems. Composed of four primary elements at the implementation level: the Common Programming Interface, Common User Access, Common Communications Support and Common Applications.

SYSTEM MESSAGE BLOCK (SMB) - Microsoft-developed protocol which allows for the movement of DOS operations across a network.

SYSTEM NETWORK ARCHITECTURE (SNA) - an IBM term referring to the formats and protocols designed by IBM to perform data communications. There are multiple layers within SNA, including physical, data-link path control, transmission control, data flow control, services management and session services.

SYSTEM NETWORK ARCHITECTURE 3270 DEVICE EMULATION - an IBM term referring to that portion of the OS/400 system which allows the AS/400 to appear like a 3274 Control Unit to a host.

SYSTEM NETWORK ARCHITECTURE BACKBONE - an IBM term referring to the family of nodes which are interconnected to run IBM's Network Control Program with 37XX products as hosts.

SYSTEM NETWORK ARCHITECTURE DATA FLOW CONTROL LAYER - refers to the fifth layer of the SNA model. The layer is responsible for features such as checkpointing, response options, pacing and queuing. The functions are very similar to the fifth layer of the OSI reference model.

SYSTEM NETWORK ARCHITECTURE DISTRIBUTION SERVICES (SNADS) - an IBM term referring to a service designed for the transfer of files, documents and electronic mail in an SNA network.

SYSTEM NETWORK ARCHITECTURE UPLINE FACILITY (SNUF) - an IBM term referring to the communications tool an AS/400 to communicate with CICS and IMS application programs running on a mainframe.

SYSTEM SERVICE CONTROL POINT (SSCP) - an IBM term used in SNA to denote a network-addressable unit which manages all or part of a network.

SYSTEM/360 - an IBM mainframe computer released in the early 1960s.

SYSTEM/370 - successor to the System/360. Released in the 1970s and still used today.

SYSTEM/390 - successor to the System/370. Released in 1990.

SYSTEM/3X - a generic term used to refer to the IBM midrange line of computers, including the System/34, System/36 and System/38.

T

TA - see *Terminal Adapter.*

TAC - see *Terminal Access Controller.*

TAIL CIRCUIT - general name for the circuit which runs between a satellite or microwave antenna and the user's ground-based equipment.

TAM - see *Telecommunications Access Method.*

TANDEM DATA CIRCUIT - circuit for transmitting which runs through two or more serially attached DTEs.

TAP - refers to the attachment of a device to a transmission medium without blocking the signal flow.

TAT - see *Turnaround Time.*

TCAM - see *Telecommunications Access Method.*

TCB - see *Transmission Control Block.*

TCM - see *Time-Compression Multiplexing.*

TCP - see *Transaction Control Process* and *Transmission Control Protocol.*

TCP/IP - see *Transmission Control Procedure/Internet Protocol.*

TCU - see *Terminal Control Unit.*

TD - see *Transmit Data.*

TDM - see *Time-Division Multiplexing.*

TDMA - see *Time-Division Multiple Access.*

TDR - see *Time Domain Reflectometer.*

TE2 - see *Terminal Equipment Type 2.*

TECHNICAL AND OFFICE PROTOCOL (TOP) - seven-layer, OSI reference model-based LAN architecture for use in office automation.

TEl - see *Terminal Equipment Type 1.*

TELECOMMUNICATIONS - the electronic transmission of information utilizing a source, a transmission medium and a receiver.

TELECOMMUNICATIONS ACCESS METHOD (TAM or TCAM) - 1) TAM--software which supplies methodologies for the transmitting and receiving of data via telecommunications circuits; 2) TCAM--an IBM term used to refer to the telecommunications access method for use in non-SNA IBM systems. TCAM manages the connection of remote devices as well as data transfer issues associated with the resulting communications session.

TELEGRAPH - transmission method which uses changes in polarity of a direct current signal to convey information. Maximum transmission speed is 75 baud.

TELEMETRY - 1) data sent from a spacecraft to a ground station; 2) transmission of data collected from sensing equipment in a real-time environment.

TELENET - the TCP/IP protocol which allows a single terminal to attach to more than one host and interact with the available applications.

TELEPRINTER - hardware device used to print telegraph messages.

TELEPROCESSING (TP) - the processing of information via telecommunications facilities.

TELETEX - ASCII-based, high-speed text transmission replacement for Telex.

TELETYPEWRITER (TTY) - hardware device used for sending and receiving messages. Obsolete.

TELEX - Baudot code-based text transmission service running at 50bps. Obsolete.

TEMPORARY TEXT DELAY (TTD) - bisync term used to indicate a character sequence which signals a temporary delay in transmission of text components within an overall message.

TENBASE-T (10BASE-T) - see Ethernet.

TERMINAL ACCESS CONTROLLER (TAC) - a network device which allows the attachment of terminal devices to the network.

TERMINAL ADAPTER (TA) - term used in ISDN to refer to the interface required for terminals incapable of attaching to an ISDN service.

TERMINAL BUFFERING - refers to the temporary storing, usually in memory, of data to be transmitted or processed.

TERMINAL CONTROL UNIT (TCU) - see *cluster controller*.

TERMINAL EMULATORS - any of the family of software which is used in a PC environrnent in order to allow the PC to act as if it were a terminal attached to the host computer.

TERMINAL EQUIPMENT TYPE 1 (TEl) - ISDN-compatible terminal family.

TERMINAL EQUIPMENT TYPE 2 (TE2) - ISDN term referring to terminals which require a TA.

TERMINAL INTERFACE PROCESSOR (TIP) - node device which permits attachment of terminals to an ARPANET network.

TERMINAL NODE (TN) - an IBM term used to designate a network node which is terminal-based.

TERMINAL SERVER - any device chartered with the task of attaching multiple terminals to an existing network.

TERMINATED LINE - condition created on a communications line when, in order to eliminate reflection, resistance is equal to line impedance.

TERMINATION - refers to a device placed in a circuit to permit terminal attachment or circuit attachment.

TERMINATOR BLOCK - the point in a building where the telephone lines terminate.

TERRESTRIAL MICROWAVE - microwave transmission scheme operating in the 1-30GHz range which uses unguided signals between towers 20-30 miles apart.

TEXT - the information (data) portion of a transmitted message.

TFTP - see *Trivial File Transfer Protocol*.

TH - see *Transmission Header*.

THICKWIRE - general term for 50-ohm, Ethernet IEEE 802.3 coaxial cable.

THIN WIRE ETHERNET - see *Cheapernet*.

THINWIRE - general term for 75-ohm, IEEE 802.3 compliant coaxial cable.

THREAD - refers to the execution path within a process.

THROUGHPUT - a measure of the amount of data which passes through a network in a specified period of time.

TI MULTIPLEXER - multiplexer for Tl lines which uses time-division multiplexing techniques.

T2 - 6.312Mbps version of Tl which supports 96 64Kbps channels.

T3 - 44.736Mbps version of Tl which supports 672 64Kbps channels.

T4 - 274.176Mbps version of Tl which supports 4,032 64Kbps channels.

TIE LINE - telephone line which connects two branch exchanges or telephone switches.

TIME DIVISION MULTIPLEXING (TDM) - device which allows multiple slow-speed devices to share a high-speed link by allocating a discrete time slice for each input device.

TIME DOMAIN REFLECTOMETER (TDR) - test device for Ethernet networks which evaluates its transmission characteristics.

TIME SHARING OPTION (TSO) - a term IBM uses to refer to its mainframe-based software package which permits multiple users to share the resources of the CPU on a percentage basis.

TIME SLICE - a measure of time allocated for a specific reason such as the processing of an instruction or the running of a program.

TIME SLOT INTERCHANGE (TSI) - term used in time-division multiplexing which refers to the swapping of assigned time slots within a frame.

TIME TO LIVE (TTL) - a value associated with the amount of time that a given datagram is allowed to remain within an internet.

TIME-COMPRESSION MULTIPLEXING (TCM) - multiplexing scheme in which modems transmit at twice their rated speed, but for only half the time of a transmission at their nominal speed (e.g., 9,600bps for 10 seconds rather than 4,800bps for 20 seconds).

TIME-DIVISION MULTIPLE ACCESS (TDMA) - multiplexing method often used in satellite technology in which multiple inputs gain access to a channel via synchronous time division multiplexing.

TIME-DIVISION MULTIPLEXING BUS SWITCHING - conceptually the same as time-division multiplexing, this scheme uses a bus with time slot allocations for switching purposes to process incoming data into a specified time slot on the bus and the output line.

TIME-DIVISION SWITCHING - see *time-division multiplexing bus switching*.

TIME-MULTIPLEXED SWITCHING (TMS) - variation of normal space-division multiplexing in which a TDM stream is composed of multiple incoming lines.

TIME-OUT INTERVAL - a measure of time allocated for a response from a receiving station by the transmitting station. If this number is reached the sender will retransmit the message or signal an error.

TIMING JITTER - refers to the variants in a carrier signal which may have been created by gain or phase changes.

TIMING SLIP - general term which describes the sudden timing delay change seen in Tl and greater transmissions due to using carriers from multiple suppliers.

TIP - see *Terminal Interface Processor.*

Tl LINES - refers to the actual physical lines which supply Tl transmission service. The TI line supports 24 64Kbps lines for a total bandwidth of 1.544Mbps.

TlC - 3.152Mbps version of Tl with capacity for 48 64Kbps channels.

TLI - see *Transport Layer Interface.*

TMS - see *Time-Multiplexed Switching.*

TN - see *Terminal Node.*

TOKEN - a specialized transmission frame used in token-passing networks to control network access. The frame normally consists of starting, ending and controlling bit sequences.

TOKEN BIT - a specific bit which identifies the message frame as being a token.

TOKEN BUS - type of local area network whose access is controlled by a rotating token in which a physical bus functions like a logical ring.

TOKEN HOLDING TIME - refers to the duration of time during which a device may transmit after it has received the access control token in a token-passing scheme network.

TOKEN PASSING - token-passing scheme allowing for distributed network management.

TOKEN ROTATION TIMER (TRT) - a measure of the duration that a token bus station has to wait until the token is passed to it.

TOKEN TREE LAN - specialized LAN design in which the topology consists of branches interconnected via active hubs which grant access by means of a token-passing mechanism.

TOKEN-RING - LAN structure which uses a physical ring and whose access is controlled by a passed token.

TOP - see *Technical and Office Protocol.*

TOP-LEVEL DOMAIN - refers to a specific, unique segment of a network used in TCP/IP UNIX environments.

TOPOLOGY - the arrangement, in a star, ring, mesh, bus, tree or hierarchical form, of nodes and links in a network.

TP - see *teleprocessing.*

TP4 - see *Transport Protocol Class Four.*

TPDU - see *Transport Protocol Data Unit.*

TRAFFIC - refers to the transmitted and received messages within a network.

TRAFFIC INTENSITY - the ratio of arrival to service rates in a network.

TRAILER - 1) the last portion of an envelope wrapped around a message frame as the frame is relocated from one protocol level to another; 2) the last portion of a message which follows the header or data portion of a given message.

TRAINING - refers to the process by which synchronous modems attain synchronization with each other.

TRANSACTION - an interchange between two devices with intent to reach a specified result.

TRANSACTION CONTROL PROCESS (TCP) - any software scheme for managing the movement of messages between application programs and network nodes.

TRANSACTION IDENTIFIER - refers to the unique identifier portion of a message in a transaction-based system.

TRANSACTION RATE - the number of transactions in a given period of time.

TRANSACTION TRACKING SYSTEM (TTS) - that portion of Novell's NetWare product which handles transaction journals and system restoration functions.

TRANSCEIVER - any device which can operate as both a transmitter and a receiver.

TRANSCEIVER CABLE - a cable used in Ethernet networks to connect a station to transceiver.

TRANSCODE - bisync character-coding methodology.

TRANSDUCER - any device which converts energy from one state to another.

TRANSFER SERVICE ACCESS POINT (TSAP) -

TRANSIENTS - unwanted electrical noise.

TRANSIT TIMING - TCP/IP term referring to a method of purging loops between the network-layer nodes.

TRANSMISSION - 1) the moving of data from one point to another; 2) the actual data being moved.

TRANSMISSION CONTROL - any of the methods used to manage the transmission of data on a network. Examples are token-passing and contention.

TRANSMISSION CONTROL BLOCK (TCB) - a data structure which holds data regarding a current TCP communication.

TRANSMISSION CONTROL LAYER SNA - an IBM term used to denote the layer whose task is the starting, maintenance, and ending of SNA sessions.

TRANSMISSION CONTROL PROCEDURE/INTERNET PROTOCOL (TCP/IP) - transport- and network-layer group of protocols developed originally for the Department of Defense. Connectionless and connection-oriented sessions are supported.

TRANSMISSION FRAME - that portion of a transmission which contains, normally, control information, error-checking data and the actual data being conveyed. The frames may be bit- or character-oriented.

TRANSMISSION GROUP - an IBM term used to denote the links between nodes in an SNA network.

TRANSMISSION HEADER (TH) - an IBM term used in SNA to indicate the data format defining the point of origin and destination of the message.

TRANSMISSION MEDIUM - refers to the physical means (e.g., coax, twinax, etc.) used to move signals.

TRANSMISSION RATE IN BITS (TRIB) - the actual number of bits transmitted across a communications channel in a given period of time. Channels may be rated for 9,600bps; but, due to propagation delay, errors, header/trailer information and so on the TRIB number will be less than 9,600. In a synchronous environment at 9,600bps, a TRIB number of 7,200bps (75 percent) should be expected.

TRANSMISSION SPEED - the rated speed for a communications channel. Contrast to *TRIB*.

TRANSMIT DATA (TD) - a pin in a cable, such as the RS-232, used to transmit data across the interface.

TRANSPARENCY - any transmission scheme which allows for the sending of data without regard to bit sequences which may be used for control purposes.

TRANSPARENT MODE - any transmission mode in which data can be sent transparently.

TRANSPARENT ROUTING - any routing scheme in which the user has no knowledge of the routing to the destination.

TRANSPARENT TEXT TRANSFER BISYNCHRONOUS TRANSMISSION - refers to the process of inserting a preceding and a trailing data-link escape character on either side of a control-character bit sequence.

TRANSPONDER - any device capable of receiving a signal, amplifying it and then retransmitting it on a different frequency.

TRANSPORT LAYER - the layer in network models responsible for network-independent, end-to-end message movement.

TRANSPORT LAYER INTERFACE (TLI) - specifications within the OSI reference model which determine the interface between the network and the transport layers.

TRANSPORT MECHANISM - generic term used to refer to any session-layer software in a network model.

TRANSPORT PROTOCOL - any protocol used in the transport layer.

TRANSPORT PROTOCOL CLASS FOUR (TP4) - a transport layer protocol defined by the ISO and embraced by the U.S. Government.

TRANSPORT PROTOCOL DATA UNIT (TPDU) - refers to the matrix into which data is formatted by a network's transport layer in order to ensure its proper use and recognition.

TRANSPORT SERVICE ACCESS POINT (TSAP) - the identification sequence that tells the upper-layer protocol entity where a protocol data unit should be delivered.

TRANSVERSE PARITY-CHECKING - a type of error-checking using a parity mechanism.

TREE - network scheme in which only one route exists between any two nodes.

TRELLIS CODE - data-coding methodology in which forward error-correction techniques are used by means of extra bits extrapolated from the message bits.

TRELLIS-CODED MODULATION - the process of encoding information on a carrier wave through the application of trellis coding.

TRIB - see *Transmission Rate in Bits*.

TRIBIT TRANSMISSION - data-transmission scheme used by some modem manufacturers in which the states of three bits are transmitted simultaneously.

TRIBUTARY STATION - also known as a slave station, this is a station on a multipoint communications line which is not the controlling (master) station.

TRIVIAL FILE TRANSFER PROTOCOL (TFTP) - basic form of TCP/IP used for file transport.

TROPOSPHERIC SCATTER - the dispersing of signals as they travel through the tropospheric portion of the atmosphere.

TRT - see *Token Rotation Timer*.

TRUNCATED BINARY EXPONENTIAL BACK-OFF - general term for the exponential back-off process used in IEEE 802.3 networks. In an exponential back-off process, the time delays increase exponentially between successive transmission attempts of a specific frame.

TRUNK AMPLIFIER - term used in broadband networking to denote a low-distortion amplifier of RF signals.

TRUNK CABLE - coaxial cable used in broadband networking for long distance distribution of RF signals.

TRUNK LINE - term used in broadband networking to denote the main cable from the headend to downstream branches.

TSAP - see *Transport Service Access Point*.

TSI - see *Time Slot Interchange*.

TSO - see *Time-Sharing Option*.

TTD - see *Temporary Text Delay*.

TTL - see *Time to Live*.

TTS - see *Transaction Tracking System*.

TTY - see *Teletypewriter*.

TURNAROUND TIME (TAT) - the time required to terminate transmission in one direction and begin transmission in another direction on a half-duplex channel.

TWA - see *Two-Way Alternate*.

TWINAX - see *Twinaxial Cable*.

TWINAXIAL CABLE (TWINAX) - a type of coaxial cable which contains two center conductors.

TWISTED WIRE PAIR (TWP) - two insulated wires twisted together to reduce noise levels; used for transmission.

TWISTED-PAIR - see twisted wire pair.

TWO-POINT CIRCUIT - another name for a point-to-point circuit.

TWO-WAY ALTERNATE (TWA) - the process of exchanging signals between two modems once a connection is established.

TWO-WAY SIMULTANEOUS TRANSMISSION - another name for full-duplex transmission.

TWP - see *Twisted Wire Pair*.

U

UA - see *User Agent.*

UART - see *Universal Asynchronous Receiver/Transmitter.*

UDP - see *User Datagram Protocol.*

UNACKNOWLEDGED CONNECTIONLESS SERVICE - a communications condition in which the LLC and MAC layers provide no acknowledgment (ACK) that data has been received, no error-recovery services and no flow control.

UNBALANCED CONFIGURATION - a network scheme utilizing primary and secondary stations functioning in a master/slave relationship.

UNBALANCED LINE - refers to the electrical state of a transmission line in which the voltage values on the two lines are not equal in respect to the ground.

UNBALANCED TRANSMISSION - transmission technique using a single conductor for signal transmission with both transmitter and receiver sharing a common ground.

UNBIND - a communications parameter requesting the deactivation of a session between two network-addressable units (NAUs).

UNBINDING - an IBM term for the process of issuing an UNBIND command in SNA.

UNBUNDLED NETWORK SERVICES - refers to the marketing of network services on an a-la-carte basis, as opposed to the services being grouped or bundled into a single package.

UNGUIDED TRANSMISSION - type of signal transmission through open space without benefit of wires or cables. Radio and most microwave transmissions are unguided.

UNICODE - a 16-bit code with 65,536 values under development by a group of computer manufacturers and intended to replace other interchange codes such as ASCII and EBCDIC.

UNIFIED NETWORK MANAGEMENT ARCHITECTURE (UNMA) - an IBM term referring to its design for network management architecture.

UNIPOLAR SIGNAL - signaling technique utilizing solely negative or positive voltages to represent the values of 1 or 0.

UNITED STATES OF AMERICA STANDARD CODE FOR INFORMATION INTERCHANGE (USASCII) - the eight-bit code standard to which most communications equipment is designed, utilizing seven data bits and a parity bit in the eighth position. There are 128 characters defined in USASCII.

UNITY GAIN - a design principle utilized in broadband networking in which the amplifiers incorporated in the network will supply sufficient signal gain at required frequencies to offset the system's signal losses.

UNIVERSAL ASYNCHRONOUS RECEIVER /TRANSMITTER (UART) - refers to an asynchronous communications entity responsible for the management of asynchronous communications employing a method that constructs words or bytes from bits and disassembles the words or bytes for transmission.

UNIVERSAL SYNCHRONOUS RECEIVER/TRANSMITTER (USRT) - communications interface used for the transmitting and receiving of information employing synchronous protocols.

UNIVERSAL SYNCHRONOUS/ASYNCHRONOUS RECEIVER/TRANSMITTER (USART) - communications interface used for devices requiring asynchronous and/or synchronous transmission and reception capabilities.

UNIX - Bell Telephone Laboratory's operating system, developed during the 1970s.

UNIX-TO-UNIX COPY PROGRAM (UUCP) - communications software designed to implement a UNIX-based international wide area network (WAN).

UNMA - see *Unified Network Management Architecture.*

UNNUMBERED FORMAT - referring to the portion of data-link protocols known as "U-frames" which are primarily used for executing special functions.

UNSHIELDED TWISTED-PAIR (UTP) - pertains to the family of communications cables which incorporate one or more pairs of twisted, insulated wires encased in an unshielded covering.

UPLINK - the communications link from a satellite's earth station to the satellite in orbit.

UPLOADING - the transferral of information from a remote location to a central location.

UPPER SIDEBAND - refers to the band of frequencies above the frequency of the carrier wave.

UPSTREAM - refers to the opposite direction of information flow in an IBM Token-Ring network.

URGENT SERVICE - TCP-provided service allowing a given application to specify transmitted data as urgent, requiring the soonest possible processing by the receiving application.

USART - see *Universal Synchronous/Asynchronous Receiver/Transmitter.*

USASCII - s e e *United States of America Standard Code for Information Interchange.*

USER AGENT (UA) - software system for interfacing the X.400 electronic mail network and a user.

USER DATAGRAM PROTOCOL (UDP) - TCP/IP networking term referring to the ability of two programs to talk directly to each other.

USER FACILITIES SERVICE - CCITT service employed in X.21 and X.25 and defined in X.2 to describe portions of the call request and call indication packets.

USER MESSAGE INTEGRITY - a phrase referring to the ability to certify that the message received is in fact the message as transmitted.

USRT - see *Universal Synchronous Receiver/Transmitter.*

UTILIIZATION - a measurement of the *actual* use of a communications line's *potential* capacity.

UTP - see *Unshielded Twisted-Pair.*

UUCP - see *UNIX-to-UNIX Copy Program.*

V

V-SERIES RECOMMENDATIONS - a series of CCITT recommendations on signaling and telecommunications standards. See Appendix G for more information.

VACC - see *Value-Added Common Carrier*.

VALIDITY-CHECKING - in data communications terminology, the proving the accuracy of transmitted data.

VALUE-ADDED COMMON CARRIER (VACC) - any common-carrier company which adds value to its basic communications offering through the offering of additional services such as least-cost routing.

VALUE-ADDED NETWORK (VAN) - a communications network offering other services besides data transmission.

VAMPIRE TAP - a type of temporary connection to a coaxial cable made without the need for cutting the cable; a vampire tap utilizes prongs to penetrate the cable and make connection with the central and outer cable conductors.

VAN - see *Value-Added Network*.

VARIABLE QUANTUM-LEVEL CODING - refers to a pulse-coded modulation scheme in which the absolute value of a pulse is encoded into a relative value.

VARIABLE-LENGTH ENCODING - bit-encoding technique in which a character is translated into a variable-length code word.

VARY OFF - the process of making unavailable a controller, line or device.

VARY ON - the process of making available a controller, line or device.

VENDOR-INDEPENDENT MESSAGING (VAM) - industry-standard messaging and mail application system created by Apple, Borland, Novell and Lotus.

VERTICAL REDUNDANCY CHECK (VRC) - error-checking routine using the parity bit of each character so that the sum of all of the 1 bits is either odd or even.

VERY HIGH FREQUENCY (VHF) - refers to frequencies in the range from 30-300MHz.

VERY LOW FREQUENCY (VLF) - refers to frequencies in the range of 3-30KHz.

VERY SMALL APERTURE TERMINAL (VSAT) - a form of wireless communications using satellites.

VHF - see *Very High Frequency*.

VIDEOTEXT - a generic term referring to an interactive telecommunications system which utilizes normal telephone lines for the transmission and reception of data.

VIM - see *Vendor-Independent Messaging*.

VIRTUAL CALL - a packet-witching network service which provides for the establishment of a virtual circuit between the sending and receiving stations which will be used for the duration of the call, even though the virtual call circuit is created before any packets are sent.

VIRTUAL CHANNEL - a communications channel giving every appearance to the locations utilizing the channel of being a permanent circuit even though it is temporary.

VIRTUAL CIRCUIT - a packet-switching network service in which a logical communications connection is made between the sending and receiving parties over which all packets are transmitted without the need for addressing information.

VIRTUAL STORAGE EXTENDED (VSE) - an IBM term referring to the operating system used on smaller members of System/370 and System/390 family of mainframes. Current versions are called VSE/ESA, with the ESA denoting Enterprise Systems Architecture.

VIRTUAL TERMINAL (VT) - applications-level protocol entity allowing applications interaction with a terminal in a constant manner, regardless of the terminal characteristics.

VIRTUAL TERMINAL ACCESS METHOD (VTAM) - an IBM term referring to the network access method utilized in SNA.

VIRTUAL TERMINAL PROTOCOLS (VTP) - generic term describing the protocols utilized for the interaction between an application and a virtual terminal.

VLF - see *Very Low Frequency*.

VM - see *VM/370*.

VM/370 - an IBM term referring to the mainframe operating system known as Virtual Machine/370. VM/370 allows for the operation of multiple "virtual machines" on the 370 and 390 series of mainframes, and each may be controlled via its own operating system.

VM/MVS BRIDGE - an IBM term referring to the network software making a bridge between an AS/400 SNADS network, a VM/370 network and an MVS network possible.

VOICE GRADE LINE - communications line with a normal bandwidth of 4KHz using the 300-3300KHz frequency range for voice transmission. Normally capable of transmitting data at rates up to and including 24,400bps, voice-grade lines may be switched or unswitched.

VOICE MAIL - a generic term referring to an electronic mail system utilizing the store-and-forward approach to data manipulation. Digitized voice messages may be created, distributed and edited using most voice-mail systems.

VOICE-OVER DATA - communications scheme in which both data and voice are transmitted over the same channel through the use of frequencies above the data-transmission bandwidth to transmit the voice signals.

VRC - see *Vertical Redundancy Check*.

VSAT - see *Very Small Aperture Terminal*.

VSE - see *Virtual Storage Extended*.

VSE/ESA - see *Virtual Storage Extended*.

VT - see *Virtual Terminal*.

VTAM - see *Virtual Terminal Access Method* (a.k.a. *Virtual Telecommunications Access Method*).

VTIOO - ASCII display station no longer in manufacture. A generic term indicating complete compliance with ANSI X3.64.

VTP - see *Virtual Terminal Protocols*.

W

WACK - see *Wait for Positive Acknowledgment.*

WAIT FOR POSITIVE ACKNOWLEDGMENT (WACK) - bisync character used to tell the transmitter that, in addition to receiving a positive acknowledgment to the last message, it should wait before transmitting the next one.

WALK TIME - a measure of the time spent moving a token or polled message from one station to the next in a token-ring or polled network, including propagation delays, modem synchronization and so forth.

WAN - see *Wide Area Network.*

WATCHDOG TIMER - refers to a device created for use in an Ethernet transceiver charged with ensuring that the size of a data frame doesn't exceed the specified maximum.

WATT - measurement of unit of power equal to 1/746th horsepower.

WAVE-DIVISION MULTIPLEXING (WDM) - multiplexing scheme utilized in fiber-optic transmissions in which multiple signals are combined onto a single optical cable.

WAVEFORM - graphical or mathematical depiction of the changes occurring to a wave over a specific span of time.

WAVEGUIDE - device used to transmit microwave data from one point to another in a constant manner.

WAVELENGTH - a measurement of the interval between two points on the same phase in adjacent cycles of a wave.

WDM - see *Wave-Division Multiplexing.*

WELL-KNOWN PORT - an Internet term denoting a TCP or UDP port number published by the Assigned Numbers Authority of Internet.

WET T1 - refers to any T1-based circuit which is attached to a telephone company-powered interface.

WIDE AREA NETWORK (WAN) - any network which has a wide geographic span.

WIDEBAND - refers to communications which occur in a bandwidth greater than 4,000Hz. Also called *broadband*.

WIDEBAND LINES - communications lines whose bandwidth is greater than 4,000Hz.

WINDOW - a measurement of the amount of data which may be transmitted before the transmitted is told to wait before sending again.

WIRE FAULT - a terminal error condition due to a break or short in a cable.

WIRING CLOSET - any room in which the wiring for communication devices is concentrated.

WORD - a term used to describe a unit of data. See *bit, byte*.

X

X MODEM - a data-link protocol developed for microcomputer systems utilizing asynchronous communications.

X SERIES RECOMMENDATIONS - the series of CCITT recommendations beginning with the letter "X" which pertain to protocols. See Appendix G for a listing.

X WINDOW SYSTEM - refers to a series of protocols originated at MIT which allow users to interact with applications which may be located at numerous computers. I/O for the applications occurs on windows of various sizes on the user's display.

XENIX - an operating system offering compatibility with PC DOS but primarily upon the UNIX operating system.

XEROX CORPORATION - a worldwide manufacturer of photocopy equipment and supplier of local area network systems.

XEROX NETWORK SYSTEM (XNS) - a local area network (LAN) scheme designed by the Xerox corporation utilizing the Ethernet standard.

XID - see *exchange identifier.*

XMIT - abbreviation for transmit.

XNS - see *Xerox Network System.*

XOFF - the equivalent of ASCII character DC3, this character is used in asynchronous communications to tell the sender to terminate transmission until an XON character is received. See *XON*.

XON - the equivalent of ASCII character DC1, this character is used in asynchronous communications to inform a sender that it may begin sending following the transmission of an XOFF. See *XOFF*.

Y-Z

YELLOW ALARM - term used in Tl communications to describe a form of transmission alarm.

ZBTSI - see *Zero-Byte Time Slot Interchange*.

ZERO CODE SUPPRESSION - any data-encoding scheme which attempts to prevent the existence of digital transmission frames which will contain eight consecutive zeros.

ZERO SLOT LOCAL AREA NETWORK - local area network scheme in which LAN cards are not needed due to the use of the serial port on the PC or workstation.

ZERO-BIT DELETION - a process found in some data-ink control protocols in which a zero is deleted from received data whenever the zero occurs after five consecutive 1 bits.

ZERO-BIT INSERTION - a process found in some data-link control protocols in which a zero is inserted into transmitted data whenever five consecutive 1 bits occur.

ZERO-BIT SUPPRESSION - denoting a methodology in which successive sequences of zero bits are guaranteed not to occur in a transmission.

ZERO-BYTE TIME SLOT INTERCHANGE (ZBTSI) - scheme used in Tl transmissions involving the dropping of a byte which is comprised of all zeros and supplying the information necessary for the receiver to recreate the byte when received at the destination.

ZERO-COMPLEMENTED DIFFERENTIAL ENCODING - see *Nonreturn to Zero Inverted* (NRZI).

Appendix A

Units of Measure

Commodity	Unit of Measure
Angle	degree, radian
Capacitance	farad
Current	ampere
Distance/Length	mile, yard, foot, inch, kilometer, meter, centimeter, millimeter
Energy	watt-second, BTU
Frequency	Hertz, cycles per second
Inductance	henry
Light	lumen, foot-candle
Loudness	decibel
Power	watt, horsepower
Resistance	ohm
Temperature	degree (Fahrenheit, Centigrade, Kelvin, Celsius)
Time	second, minute, hour
Voltage	volt
Weight	ton, pound, ounce, kilogram, gram, centigram, milligram

Appendix B

Conversions

From	To	Multiply by
BTJ	kilowatt-hour	0.0002928
centimeters	inches	0.3937
degrees	radians	0.01731
feet	meters	0.3048
feet	inches	12
horsepower	watts	745.7
hours	minutes	60
hours	seconds	3600
inches	centimeters	2.54
inches	mils	1000
kilowatt-hour	BTU	3415.3
radians	degrees	57.78237
meters	feet	3.2808
mils	inches	0.001
watts	horsepower	0.001341

Appendix C

American Wire Gauge Sizes and Resistances

Gauge	Diameter (inches)	Area (sq. In)	Ohms/1000 Ft (70 F)
10	0.102	.008172	1.02
11	0.091	.006504	1.29
12	0.081	.005153	1.62
13	0.072	.004072	2.04
14	0.064	.003217	2.57
15	0.057	.002552	3.24
16	0.051	.002043	4.10
17	0.045	.001590	5.15
18	0.040	.001257	6.51
19	0.036	.001018	8.21
20	0.032	.000804	10.30
21	0.028	.000616	13.00
22	0.025	.000491	16.50
23	0.024	.000452	20.70
24	0.020	.000314	26.20
25	0.018	.000254	33.00
26	0.016	.000201	41.80
27	0.014	.000154	52.40
28	0.013	.000133	66.60
29	0.011	.000095	82.80

Appendix D

Magnitude Prefixes

Prefix	Magnitude	Abbreviation	Example
exa-	10(18)	E	EXAwatts
peta-	10(15)	P	PETAseconds
tera-	10(12)	T	TERAwatts
giga-	10(9)	G	GIGAbytes
mega-	10(6)	M	MEGAcycles
kilo-	10(3)	k	Kilowatts
hect6-	10(2)	h	HECTOradians
deka-	10	da	DEKAliters
deci-	10(-1)	d	DECIohms
centi-	10(-2)	c	CENTImeters
milli-	10(-3)	m	MILLIliters
micro-	10(-6)		MICROseconds
nano-	10(-9)	n	NANOseconds
pico-	10(-12)	p	PICOvolts

Appendix E

Electronic Industries Association (EIA) RS-232 Modem-terminal Interface

Pin	Name	To Dte	To Dce	Function	Eia Circuit
1	FG			Frame Ground	(AA)
2	TD		y	Transmitted Beta	(BA)
3	RD	y		Received Data	(BB)
4	RTS		y	Request To Send	(CA)
5	CT	y		Clear To Send	(CB)
6	DSR	y		Beta Set Ready	(CC)
7	SG			Signal Ground	(AB)
8	DCD	y		Data Carrier Detect	(CF)
9		y		Positive DC Test Voltage	
10		y		Negative DC Test Voltage	
11	QM	y		Equalizer Mode Bell 208A	
12	DCD	y		Sec. Data Carrier Detect	(SCF)
13	CTS	y		Sec. Clear To Send	(SCB)
14	TD		y	Sec. Transmitted Data	(SBA)
	NS		y	New Sync	
15	TC	y		Transmitter Clock	(DB)
16	RD	y		Sec. Received Data	(SBB)
	DCT	y		Divided Clock Xmitter	
17	RC	y		Receiver Clock	(DD)
18	DCR	y		Divided Clock Receiver	
19	RTS		y	Sec. Request to Send	(SCA)
20	DTR		y	Data Terminal Ready	(CD)
21	SO	y		Signal Quality Detect	(CG)
22	RI	y		Ring Indicator	(CE)
23			y	Data Rate Selector	(CH)
		y		Data Rate Selector	(CI)
24	TC		y	Ext. Xmitter Clock	(DA)

Appendix F:
Commonly Referenced Standards Organizations

AMERICAN NATIONAL STANDARDS INSTITUTE (ANSI)
1430 Broadway
New York, NY 10010
(212) 354-3471

CONSULTATIVE COMMITTEE ON INTERNATIONAL
TELEPHONY AND TELEGRAPH (CCITT)
General Secretariat - International Telecommunications Union
Place des Nations
1211 Geneva 20 Switzerland

ELECTRONIC INDUSTRIES ASSOCIATION (EIA)
2001 Eye Street, N.W.
Washington, DC 20006
(202) 457-4966

INSTITUTE OF ELECTRICAL AND ELECTRONIC ENGINEERS (IEEE)
345 East 47th Street
New York, NY 10017
(212) 705-7900

INTERNATIONAL ORGANIZATION FOR STANDARDIZATION (ISO)
Central Secretariat
1, Rue de Varembe
1204 Geneva, Switzerland
22) 34.12.40

Appendix G:

Selected Major Standards And Recommendations

Selected CCITT G-series Recommendations

These selected G-series recommendations relate to transmission systems and multiplexing equipment characteristics of digital networks.

G.701	General structure of the G.700, G.800 recommendations.
G.702	Terminology used for pulse code modulation (PCM) and digital transmission.
G.703	General aspects of interfaces.
G.704	Maintenance of digital networks.
G.705	Integrated Services Digital Network (ISDN).
G.711	PCM of voice frequencies.
G.712	Performance characteristics of PCM channels at audio frequencies.
G.721	Hypothetical reference of digital paths.
G.722	Interconnection of digital paths using different techniques.
G.731	Primary PCM multiplex equipment for voice frequencies.
G.732	Characteristics of primary PCM multiplex equipment operating at 2,048Kbps.
G.733	Characteristics of primary PCM multiplex equipment operating at 1,544Kbps.
G.734	Frame structure for use with digital exchanges at 2,048Kbps.
G.735	Termination of 1,544Kbps digital paths on digital exchanges.
G.736	Characteristics of synchronous digital multiplex equipment operating at 1,544Kbps.
G.737	Characteristics of primary PCM multiplex equipment operating at 2,048Kbps and offering synchronous 64Kbps digital access options.
G.738	Characteristics of synchronous digital multiplex equipment operating at 2,048Kbps.

181

G.739	Characteristics of external access equipment operating at 2,048Kbps and offering synchronous digital access at 64Kbps.
G.741	General considerations on second-order multiplex equipment.
G.742	Second-order digital multiplex equipment operating at 8,448Kbps and using positive justification.
G.743	Second-order digital multiplex equipment operating at 6,312Kbps and using positive justification.
G.744	Second-order PCM multiplex equipment operating at 8,448Kbps.
G.745	Second-order digital multiplex equipment operating at 8,448Kbps and using positive/zero/negative justification.
G.746	Frame structure for use with digital exchanges at 8,448Kbps.
G.751	Digital multiplex equipment operating at third-order bit rates of 34,368Kbps and fourth-order bit rates of 139,264Kbps and using positive justification.
G.752	Characteristics of digital multiplex equipment based on second-order bit rates of 6,312Kbps and using positive justification.
G.753	Third-order digital multiplex equipment operating at 34,368Kbps and using positive/zero/negative justification.
G.754	Fourth-order digital multiplex equipment operating at 139,264Kbps and using positive/zero/negitive justification.
G.791	General considerations for transmultiplexing equipment.
G.792	Characteristics common to all transmultiplexing equipment.
G.793	Characteristics of 60-channel transmultiplexing equipment.

Selected CCITT I-series Recommendations

These selected I-series recommendations all relate to Integrated Services Digital Networks (ISDNs).

I.100	General ISDN concepts.
I.110	General structure of the I-series recommendations.
I.111	Relationship with other recommendations relevant to ISDNs.
I.112	Vocabulary of terms for ISDNs.
I.113	Vocabulary of terms for broadband ISDNs.
I.120	ISDN description.

I.121	Broadband ISDNs.
I.122	Framework for providing additional packet-mode bearer services.
I.130	Method for the characterization of telecommunications services supported by an ISDN network.
I.140	Attribute technique for the characterization of telecommunications services supported by ISDNs.
I.141	ISDN network-charging capabilities attributes.
I.200	Service features for ISDNs.
I.210	Principles of telecommunications services supported by an ISDN.
I.211	Bearer services supported by an ISDN.
I.212	Teleservices supported by an ISDN.
I.220	Common dynamic description of basic telecommunications services.
I.221	Common specific characteristics of telecommunications services.
I.230	Definition of bearer services categories.
I.231	Circuit-mode bearer service categories.
I.232	Packet-mode bearer service categories.
I.240	Definition of teleservices supported by ISDN.
I.241	Service descriptions of teleservices supported by ISDN.
I.250	Definition of supplementary services in ISDN.
I.251	Number identification supplementary services.
I.252	Call offering supplementary services.
I.253	Call completion supplementary services.
I.254	Multiparty supplementary services.
I.255	Community of interest supplementary services.
I.256	Changing supplementary services.
I.257	Additional information transfer supplementary services.
I.300	Network features for ISDN.
I.310	ISDN network function principles.
I.320	ISDN protocol reference model.
I.32x	ISDN architecture function model.
I.32y	ISDN hypothetical reference connections.

I.330	ISDN numbering and addressing principles.
I.331	ISDN numbering plan.
I.33x	ISDN routing principles.
I.340	ISDN connection types.
I.35x	ISDN performance objectives relating to circuit-switched connections.
I.35y	ISDN performance objectives related to packet-switched connections.
I.400	ISDN network/user interface features.
I.410	General aspects and principles relating to recommendations on ISDN user network interfaces.
I.411	ISDN user network interfaces, reference configuration.
I.412	ISDN user network interfaces, channel structures and access capabilities.
I.420	Basic access user network interface.
I.421	Primary rate user access interface.
I.430	Basic user network interface, layer 1 specifications.
I.431	Primary rate user network interface, layer 1 specifications.
I.43x	Higher rate user network interface.
I.440	ISDN user network interface, layer 2 general aspects.
I.441	ISDN user network interface data link specifications.
I.450	Layer 3, general aspects.
I.451	ISDN layer 3 specifications.
I.452	Procedures for control of ISDN supplementary services.
I.460	Multiplexing, rate adaptation and support of existing interfaces.
I.461	Support of X.21- and X.21bis-based DTEs by an ISDN (X.30).
I.462	Support of packet-mode terminal equipment by an ISDN (X.31).
I.463	Support of DTEs with V-series type interfaces by an ISDN.
I.464	Rate adaptation and multiplexing support of existing interfaces for restricted 64Kbps transfer capability.
I.465	Support of DTEs with V-series interfaces with provisions for statistical multiplexing.
I.500	Internetwork interfaces for ISDN.

I.510   ISDN internetworking, general principles.

I.511   ISDN-to-ISDN layer 1 internetworking interface.

I.515   Parameter exchange for ISDN internetworking.

I.520   General arrangements for internetworking between ISDNs.

I.530   Network internetworking between ISDN and Public Switched Telephone Network.

I.540   Internetworking between circuit-switched PDNs and ISDNs.

I.550   Internetworking between packet-switched PDNs and ISDNs.

I.560   Requirements to be met providing telex service within ISDNs.

I.600/605   Maintenance requirements for ISDNs.

Selected CCITT V-series Recommendations

The following V-series recommendations refer to data transmission over telephone networks.

V.1   Equivalence between binary notation symbols and the significant conditions of a two-condition cable.

V.2   Power levels for data transmission over telephone lines.

V.3   International Alphabet number 5.

V.4   General structure of signals of international alphabet number 5 code for data transmission over public telephone networks.

V.5   Standards of modulation rates and data signaling rates for synchronous data transmission in the general switched network.

V.6   Standards of modulation rates and data signaling rates for synchronous data transmission on leased-line circuits.

V.7   Definition of terms concerning data transmission over the telephone network.

V.10   Electrical characteristics for unbalanced double current interchange circuits for general use with integrated circuit equipment in the field of data communications (RS-423).

V.11   Electrical characteristics for balanced double current interchange circuits for general use with integrated circuit equipment in the field of data communications (RS-422).

V.13   Answerback unit simulator.

V.15   Use of acoustic coupling or data transmission.

V.16	Recommendations or modems for the transmission of medical dialogue data.
V.19	Modems for parallel data transmission using signaling frequencies.
V.20	Parallel data transmission modems standardized for universal use in the general switched network.
V.21	300bps modem standardized for use in the switched telephone network.
V.22	1,200bps, full-duplex, two-wire modem standardized for use on the general switched telephone network and for leased lines.
V.22bis	2,400bps, full-duplex, two-wire modem using frequency-division scheme standardized for use in switched telephone network.
V.23	600/1,200bps modem standardized for use in the general switched telephone network.
V.24	List of definitions for interchange circuits between data terminal equipment (DTE) and data circuit-terminating equipment (DCE) (RS-232C).
V.25	Automatic calling/answering equipment on the general switched telephone network including disabling echo-suppressors on manually established calls.
V.25bis	Automatic calling/answering equipment on the general switched telephone network using the 100-series interchange circuits.
V.26	2,400bps modem for use on four-wire leased point-to-point telephone circuits.
V.26bis	2,400/1,200bps modem standardized for use in the general switched telephone network.
V.26ter	2,400bps duplex modem using echo cancellation standardized for use in the general switched telephone network and on point-to-point, two-wire, leased telephone circuits.
V.27	4,800bps modem with manual equalizer standardized for use on leased telephone circuits.
V.27bis	4,800/2,400bps modem with automatic equalizer standardized for use on leased circuits.
V.27ter	4,800/2,400 bpsmodem with automatic equalizer standardized for use on the general switched telephone network.
V.28	Electrical characteristics for unbalanced double-current interchange circuits.

V.29	9,600bps modem standardized for use on leased circuits.
V.31	Electrical characteristics for single-current interchange circuits controlled by contact closure.
V.31bis	Electrical characteristics for single-current interchange circuits using optocouplers.
V.32	Duplex modems operating at data rates of up to 9,600bps standardized for use in the general switched telephone network and in two-wire leased telephone circuits.
V.33	Full-duplex synchronous or asynchronous transmission at 14,400Kbps for use in the public telephone network.
V.35	Interface between DTEs and DCEs using electrical signal defined in V.11 (RS-449).
V.36	Modems for synchronous data transmission using 60-108KHz group band circuits.
V.37	Synchronous data transmission at data rates in excess of 72Kbps using 60-108KHz group band circuits.
V.40	Error indication with electromagnetic equipment.
V.41	Code-independent error control system.
V.42	Modem error-detection and -correction scheme.
V.42bis	Data-compression method used with V.42.
V.50	Standard limits for transmission quality for data transmission.
V.51	Organization of the maintenance of international telephone circuits used for data transmission.
V.52	Characteristics of distortion and error-rate measuring apparatus for data transmission.
V.53	Limits for the maintenance of telephone circuits used for data transmission.
V.54	Loop test device for modems.
V.55	Specifications for an impulsive noise-measuring instrument for telephone circuits.
V.56	Comparative tests for modems used on telephone circuits.
V.57	Comprehensive data test set for high signaling rates.
V.100	Interconnection between PDNs and public switched telephone network.
V.110	Support of DTEs with V-series interfaces by an ISDN (I.463).

V.120	Support by ISDN of DTEs with V-series interfaces with provision for statistical multiplexing.
V.230	General data communications interface layer 1 specifications.

Selected CCITT X-series Recommendations

The following selected X-series recommendations refer to public data network architecture.

X.1	International user classes of service in public data networks (PDNs) and ISDN.
X.2	International user facilities in PDNs.
X.3	Packet assembly/disassembly facility in PDNS.
X.3.4	ANSI standard for 7-bit information code.
X.3.15	ANSI specifications for bit sequencing of the X3.4 code in serial data streams.
X.3.16	ANSI specifications for character and parity structure in X3.4 transmissions.
X.3.28	ANSI standard for control characters.
X.3.41	ANSI specifications for code extensions using 7-bit X3.4.
X.3.66	ANSI definition of Advanced Data Communications Control Procedures (ADCCP).
X.4	General structure of signals in international alphabet number 5 code for data transmission in PDNs.
X.10	Categories for access of DTEs to public data transmission services.
X.15	Definition of terms concerning PDNs.
X.20	Interface between DTEs and DCEs for start-stop transmission over PDNs.
X.20bis	V.21-compatible interface between DTEs and DCEs for start-stop transmision services on PDNs.
X.21	General-purpose interface between DTEs and DCEs for synchronous operations on PDNs.
X.21bis	Use on PDNs of DTEs which are designed for interfacing to synchronous V-series modems.
X.22	Multiplex DTE/DCE equipment for user classes 3-6.
X.24	Lists of definitions of interchange circuits between DTEs and DCEs on PDNs.

X.25	Interfaces for DTEs and DCEs operating in packet-mode on PDNS.
X.26	Electrical characteristics for unbalanced double-current interchange circuits for general use with integrated circuit equipment in data communications (V.10).
X.27	Electrical characteristics for balanced double-current interchange circuits for general use with integrated circuit equipment in data communications (V.11).
X.28	DTE/DCE equipment interface for start/stop mode DTEs accessing the packet assembly/disassembly (PAD) facility on a PDN in the same country.
X.29	Procedures for exchange of control information and user data between a packet-mode DCE and a PAD facility.
X.30	Support of X.21- and X.21bis-based DTEs by an ISDN (I.461).
X.31	Support of packet-mode terminal equipment by an ISDN (I.462).
X.32	Interface between DTEs and DCEs for terminals operating in packet mode and accessing packet-switched PDN through a public switched network (PSN).
X.40	Standardization of frequency-shift and modulated transmission systems.
X.50	Fundamental parameters of a multiplexing scheme for the international interface between synchronous data networks.
X.50bis	Fundamental parameters of a 48Kbps user data signaling rate transmission scheme for the international interface between synchronous data networks.
X.51	Fundamental parameters of a multiplexing scheme for the international interface between synchronous data networks using 10-bit envelope structure.
X.51bis	Fundamental parameters of a 48Kbps user data signaling rate transmission scheme for the international interface between synchronous data networks using 10-bit envelope structure.
X.52	Method of encoding asynchronous signals into a synchronous user bearer.
X.53	Number of channels on international multiplex links at 64Kbps.
X.54	Allocation of channels on international multiplex links at 64Kbps.
X.55	Interface between synchronous data networks using a 6 + 2 envelope structure and single channel per carrier satellite channels.

X.56	Interface between synchronous data networks using an 8 + 2 envelope structure and single channel per carrier satellite channels.
X.57	Method of transmitting a single lower-speed data channel on a 64Kbit data stream.
X.58	Parameters of a multiplexing scheme for the international interface between synchronous, nonswitched data networks using no envelope structure.
X.60	Common channel signaling for channel-switched data applications.
X.61	Signaling system number 7 (data user portion).
X.70	Terminal and transit control signaling system on international circuits between asynchronous data networks.
X.71	Decentralized terminal and transit control signaling system on international circuits between synchronous data networks.
X.75	Terminal and transit call control procedures and data transfer systems on international circuits between packet-switched data networks.
X.80	Internetworking of interexchange signaling for circuit-switched data services.
X.81	Internetworking between an ISDN circuit-switched and a circuit-switched PDN.
X.82	Internetworking between circuit-switched PDNs and public-service PDNs.
X.87	Principles and procedures for realization of international test facilities and network utilities in PDNs.
X.92	Hypothetical reference connections for public synchronous data networks.
X.95	Network parameters in PDNs.
X.96	Call progress signals in PDNs.
X.110	Routing principles for international public data services through switched PDNs of the same type.
X.121	International numbering plans for PDNs.
X.130	Provisional objectives for call setup and clear-down times in public synchronous data networks.
X.131	Call blocking in PDNs when providing international synchronous circuit-switched data service.

X.132	Provisional objectives for grade of service in international data communications over switched-circuit PDNs.
X.134	Portion boundaries and packet-layer reference events.
X.135	Speed of service performance values for PDNs in international PDNs.
X.136	Accuracy and dependability performance values for PDNs in international PDNS.
X.137	Availability performance values for PDNs when in international PDNs.
X.140	General quality of service parameters for PDNS.
X.141	General principles for error detection/correction in PDNS.
X.150	DTE and DCE test loops for PDNs.
X.180	Administration arrangements for international closed user groups.
X.181	Administrative arrangements for international permanent virtual circuits.

This series of X-recommendations are in reference to OSI and Internetworking

X.200	Reference model of Open Systems Interconnection (OSI) for CCITT applications.
X.210	OSI layer service definition conventions.
X.211	Physical service definition for OSI model for CCITT applications.
X.212	Data-link service definition for OSI for CCITT applications.
X.213	Network service definition for OSI for CCITT applications.
X.214	Transport service definition for OSI for CCITT applications.
X.215	Session service definition for OSI for CCITT applications.
X.216	Presentation services definition for OSI for CCITT applications.
X.217	Association control services definition for OSI for CCITT applications.
X.218	Reliable transfer: definitions.
X.219	Remote operation: definitions.
X.220	Use of X.200 series protocols in CCITT applications.
X.223	Use of X.25 protocols to provide OSI network services for CCITT applications.
X.224	Transport protocol specifications for OSI for CCITT applications.

X.225	Session protocol specifications for OSI for CCITT applications.
X.226	Presentation protocol specifications for OSI for CCITT applications.
X.227	Association control specifications for OSI for CCITT applications.
X.228	Reliable transfer protocol specifications.
X.229	Remote operations protocol specifications.
X.244	Procedure for the exchange of protocol identical during virtually all establishment on packet-switched PDNs.
X.250	Formal description techniques for data communications protocols and services.
X.300/302	General principles for internetworking between public networks and/or other networks.
X.305	Functions of subnetworks relating to OSI support.
X.320	Internetworking between ISDNs.
X.321	Internetworking between circuit-switched PDNs and ISDNs.
X.322	Internetworking between packet-switched PDNs (PSPDNs) and circuit-switched PDNs (CSPDNs).
X.323	Internetworking between PSPDNs.
X.324	Internetworking between PSPDNs and public mobile systems.
X.325	Internetworking between PSPDNs and ISDNs.
X.326	Internetworking between PSPDNs and common channel signaling networks.
X.327	Internetworking between PSPDNs and private data networks.
X.350	Internetworking requirements, public mobile data systems.
X.351	Special requirements for PADs in association with earth stations in public mobile satellite services.
X.352	Internetworking between PSPDNs and public maritime mobile satellite systems.
X.353	Routing principles for interconnecting public maritime systems and PDNs.
X.370	Arrangements for the transfer of internetworking management information.
X.400/420	Message handling service for all test communications and electronic mail.

X.500/521 Specifications defining universal interconnectivity of public electronic mail networks.

Selected Electronic Industries Association (EIA) Standards

EIA-RS-232	Interface between DTEs and DCEs using serial binary data exchange.
EIA-RS-269	Synchronous signaling rates for data transmission. (X.3.1).
EIA-RS-334	Signal quality at interface between DTEs and synchronous DCEs for serial transmission.
EIA-RS-357	Interface between facsimile terminal equipment and voice-frequency DTEs.
EIA-RS-363	Standard for specifying signal quality for transmitting and receiving DTEs using serial data transmission at the interface with the asynchronous DCEs.
EIA-RS-366	Interface between DTEs and automatic calling equipment.
EIA-RS-404	Standard for start/stop signal quality between DTEs and asynchronous DCES.
EIA-RS-408	Interface between numerical control equipment and DTEs using binary data interchange (parallel).
ElA-RS-410	Standard for electrical characteristics of Class A closure interchange circuits.
EIA-RS-422	Electrical characteristics of balanced voltage digital interface circuits.
EIA-RS-423	Electrical characteristics of unbalanced voltage digital interface circuits.
EIA-RS-442	Variation of EIA-RS-449 interface.
EIA-RS-443	Variation of EIA-RS-449 interface.
EIA-RS-449	Specifications for 37-position interface for DTEs and DCEs using serial binary data interchange (see also EIA-RS-422, EIA-RS-423).
EIA-RS-470	Telephone instruments with loop signaling. Technical criteria for connecting various equipment to the public telephone network.

EIA-RS-484	Interface characteristics and line control protocol with control characters for serial data link between direct numerical control systems and numerical control equipment with asynchronous full-duplex transmission.
EIA-RS-485	Standard for electrical characteristics of generators and receivers for use in balanced digital multipoint systems.
EIA-RS-491	Interface between a numerical control unit and peripheral equipment employing asynchronous binary data interchange over circuits with EIA-423 electrical characteristics.
EIA-RS-496	Interface between DCEs and the public switched telephone network.
EIA-530	High-speed 25-pin interface between DTEs and DCEs.
EIA-536	General aspects of Group 4 facsimile equipment.
EIA-537	Control procedures for telematic terminals.
EIA/TIA-568	Standards for commercial-building wiring schemes.

Selected Institute Of Electrical And Electronic Engineers (IEEE) Standards

IEEE 488	General-purpose bus-interface definitions.
IEEE 802.1	Local area network (LAN) internetworking standard.
IEEE 802.2	LAN logical link control layer standard.
IEEE 802.3	LAN standard for Carrier Sense Multiple Access with Collision Detect (CSMA/CD).
IEEE 802.4	LAN standard for token bus.
IEEE 802.5	LAN standard for token-ring.
IEEE 802.6	LAN standard for metropolitan area networks (MANs).
IEEE 1003	Definition of portable operating systems.

Selected International Standards Organization (ISO) Standards

ISO 646	Seven-bit character set for information processing.
ISO 1155	Use of longitudinal parity to detect errors.
ISO 1177	Character structure for start/stop and synchronous transmissions.
ISO 1745	Basic mode control procedures.
ISO 2022	Code extension scheme for ISO seven-bit character set.
ISO 2110	Specifications for 25-pin DTE-to-DCE interface.
ISO 2111	Mode control procedures for code-independent data transfer.
ISO 2375	Procedure for registration of escape sequences.
ISO 2593	Connector pin allocations for high-speed DTEs.
ISO 2628	Basic mode control procedures.
ISO 2629	Basic mode control procedures for conversational message transfer.
ISO 3309	High-Level Data-Link Control (HDLC) procedures.
ISO 4335	HDLC procedures.
ISO 4902	Specifications for 27-pin DTE-to-DCE interface.
ISO 4903	Specifications for 15-pin DTE-to-DCE interface.
ISO 5218	Information exchange: representation of human sexes.
ISO 6159	HDLC unbalanced classes of procedures.
ISO 6256	HDLC balanced classes of procedures.
ISO 6429	Control functions for seven- and eight-bit character sets.
ISO 6523	Structures for identification of organizations.
ISO 6937-1	General information on coded-character sets for text communications.
ISO 7477	Description of wiring scheme for null modems.
ISO 7478	Data communications: multilink procedures.
ISO 7480	Start/stop signal transmission quality at DTE/DCE interfaces.
ISO 7498	OSI reference model.

ISO 7776	Description of X.25 LAPB-compatible DTE data-link procedures.
ISO 7809	HDLC consolidation of classes of procedures.
ISO 8072	Transport-layer definitions for OSI model.
ISO 8073	Specifications for transport layer of seven OSI networks.
ISO 8208	Specifications for lower three layers of OSI model for packet-switching networks (X.25).
ISO 8326/8327	Specifications for session-layer services in circuit-switched OSI networks.
ISO 8348	Circuit-switching standards.
ISO 8348 - AD1	Network-layer packet-switching process specifications.
ISO-8348 - AD2	Network-layer address-format specifications.
ISO 8472/8473	Network layer of OSI packet-switched network.
ISO 8480	DTE/DCE interface backup using 25-pin connector.
ISO 8481	DTE-to-DTE connection using X.24 interchange circuits with DTE-provided timing.
ISO 8482	Twisted-pair multipoint interconnections.
ISO 8509	OSI: service conventions.
ISO 8571	File access and transfer in OSI networks.
ISO 8602/8072	Transport-layer services in OSI networks using connectionless service.
ISO 8613	Document content architecture and interchange format.
ISO 8632	ISO definition of Computer Graphics Metafile (CGM).
ISO 8648	Network-layer internal organization of OSI model.
ISO 8649/8650	Application-layer standard covering various protocol issues.
ISO 8802.2	ISO version of IEEE 802.2
ISO 8802.3	ISO version of IEEE 802.3.
ISO 8802.4	ISO version of IEEE 802.4
ISO 8802.5	ISO version of IEEE 802.5.
ISO 8822/8823	Presentation-layer standards for use with circuit-switched services.
ISO 8832/8833	Definitions for Job Transfer and Manipulation (JTM) applications.

ISO 8878	X.25 as a connection-oriented service.
ISO 8880	Protocol combinations to support OSI services.
ISO 8881	Network-layer standard covering X.25 usage in LANs.
ISO 8885	General-purpose XID frame information.
ISO 8886	Data-link layer definitions in OSI model.
ISO 9036	Data-link service definitions for OSI.
ISO 9040/9041	Application-layer standard on virtual terminal services protocols.
ISO 9066	Reliable transfer: service/protocol definitions.
ISO 9067	Automatic fault-isolation procedures using test loops.
ISO 9072	Remote operations model/protocols.
ISO 9314-1	Physical-layer standard covering protocol issues in medium-independent Fiber Distributed Data Interface (FDDI) systems.
ISO 9314-2	Data-link layer standard covering medium access control protocols in FDDI.
ISO 9314-3	Physical layer standard covering transmission protocols in medium-independent FDDI.
ISO 9542	End system-to-intermediate system routing-exchange protocol for use in conjunction with protocol providing connectionless service.
ISO 9543	Synchronous transmission signal quality at DCE/DTE interface.
ISO 9545	OSI application-layer structure.
ISO 9548	Session-layer connectionless service for OSI model.
ISO 9574	OSI connection-mode network service by packet mode terminal equipment and ISDN.
ISO 9575	OSI routing framework.
ISO 9576	Presentation-layer connectionless service for OSI model.
ISO 9577	Protocol ID in the network layer.
ISO 9578	Communications connections interfaces in LANs.
ISO 9579	Application-layer standard covering remote database access services.
ISO 9594	Application-layer standard covering directory services in electronic mail (X.500).

ISO 9595 — OSI common management services definitions.

ISO 9596 — Application-layer standard covering network management communications in lower layers of OSI model.

ISO 10020/10021 Application-layer standard covering message-handling in electronic mail systems (X.400).

ISO 10026 — Standard for Distributed Transaction Processing (DTP).

ISO 10029 — Operations of an X.25 internetworking unit.

ISO 10589 — Network-layer standard covering ISIS system transfer processes.

Selected American National Standards Institute (ANSI) Standards

ANSI Tl.101-1987	Synchronous interface standards for digital networks.
ANSI Tl.102-1987	Digital hierarchy: electrical interfaces.
ANSI Tl.103-1987	Digital hierarchy: synchronous DS3 format specifications.
ANSI TI.105-1988	Digital hierarchy: optical interface rates and format specifications.
ANSI Tl.106-1988	Digital hierarchy: optical interface specifications (single mode).
ANSI Tl.107-1988	Digital hierarchy: format specifications.
ANSI Tl.110-1987	Supplement to TI.107-1988.
ANSI Tl.111-1987	Signaling system 7: general information.
ANSI Tl.112-1988	Signaling system 7: signaling connection.
ANSI Tl.113-1988	Signaling system 7: ISDN user part.
ANSI Tl.114-1988	Signaling system 7: transaction capability applications part.
ANSI Tl.115-1989	Monitoring/measuring in signaling system 7 networks.
ANSI Tl.116-1989	Signaling system 7: operations, maintenance and administration.
ANSI Tl.219-1991	ISDN management: overview and principles.
ANSI Tl.308-1990	ISDN customer installation: metallic interfaces layer 1 specification.

ANSI T1.601-1988	ISDN basic access interface for use on metallic loops for application on the network side of layer 1 specifications.
ANSI TI.602-1989	ISDN data-link layer signaling specifications for application at the user-network interface.
ANSI T1.603-1990	Minimal set of bearer services for ISDN primary rate interface.
ANSI T1.604-1990	Minimal set of bearer standards for the ISDN basic rate interface.
ANSI T1.605-1989	ISDN basic access interface for S&T reference points.
ANSI T1.606-1990	ISDN architectural framework and service description for frame-relay bearer service.
ANSI T1.607-1990	ISDN layer 3 signaling specification for circuit-switched bearer service for digital subscriber signaling system number 1.
ANSI TI.609-1990	Internetworking between ISDN user-network internetwork interface protocol and signaling system 7 ISDN user part.
ANSI T1.610-1990	Digital subscriber signaling system 1: generic procedures for the control of ISDN supplementary services.
ANSI T1.611-1991	Signaling system 7 : supplementary services for non-ISDN subscribers.
ANSI T1.613-1991	ISDN call-waiting supplementary service.
ANSI X3.1-1987	Data transmission: synchronous signaling rates.
ANSI X3.4-1986	Specifications for seven-bit American Standard Code for Information Interchange (ASCII).
ANSI X3.6-1965	Revised 1983: Perforated tape code for information interchange.
ANSI X3.15-1976	Revised 1983: Bit sequence of ASCII serial-by-bit data transmision.
ANSI X3.16-1976	Revised 1983: Character structure and character parity sense for serial-by-bit data communications in ASCII.
ANSI X3.25-1976	Revised 1983: same as ANSI 3.16 except for "parallel-by-bit".

ANSI X3.28-1976	Revised 1986: use procedures for control characters in ASCII.
ANSI X3.32-1990	Graphic representation of ASCII control characters.
ANSI X3.41-1990	Code extension schemes for ASCII.
ANSI X3.44-1990	Determination of the performance of data communications systems.
ANSI X3.57-1977	Revised 1986: message heading structures with ASCII.
ANSI X3.64-1979	Revised 1990: additional controls for ASCII use.
ANSI X3.66-1979	Revised 1990: Advanced Data Communications Control Procedures (ADCCP).
ANSI X3.79-1981	Determination of performance of data communications systems that use bit-oriented communications control procedures.
ANSI X3.92-1981	Revised 1987: data-encryption algorithm.
ANSI X3.100-1989	DTE/DCE interface in PSDNs or between two DTEs, by dedicated circuit.
ANSI X3.102-1983	Revised 1990: data communications user-oriented performance parameters.
ANSI X3.105-1983	Revised 1990: data-link encryption.
ANSI X3.106-1983	Revised 1990: modes of operation for data-encryption algorithm.
ANSI X3.108-1988	Local distributed data interface: physical-layer interface to nonbranching coaxial cable bus.
ANSI X3.139-1987	FDDI: token-ring medium access control (MAC).
ANSI X3.140-1986	OSI: connection-oriented, transport-layer protocol specification.
ANSI X3.141-1987	Measurement methods for user-oriented performance evaluation.
ANSI X3.148	FDDI token-ring physical-layer protocol.
ANSI X3.153-1987	OSI: basic connection-oriented, session-protocol specifications.
ANSI X3.166-1990	FDDI: physical-layer medium dependent.

Appendix H:
Commonly Used North American Carrier Systems

Digital Multiplex Carrier Systems

Signal Name	Medium Name	Medium Type**	Multiplex Name	Transfer Rate	Voice Channels
DS-1	T1	T/P	D-Channel	1.544Mbps	24
DS-1C	T1C	T/P	M1C	3.152Mbps	48
DS-2	T2	T/P	M12	6.312Mbps	96
DS-3	FT-3	F/O	M13	44.74Mbps	672
DS-4	TM4	C/C	M34	274.18Mbps	4032
	FT4	F/O	M34	274.18Mbps	4032

Analog Multiplex Carrier Systems

Signal Name	Bandwidth of Signal	Medium Type	Voice Channels
K	300KHz	T1P	12
N1	300KHz	T/P	12
N2	300KHz	T/P	12
N3	300KHz	T/P	24
N4	300KHz	T/P	24
L1	3MHz	C/C	1800
L3	10MHz	C/C	9300
L	420MHz	C/C	32400
L5	68MHz	C/C	10800

** T/P = twisted-pair
F/O = fiber-optic
C/C = coaxial cable

AS/400 Communications Desk Reference